SWING
AND
EARLY PROGRESSIVE
PIANO STYLES

SWING AND EARLY PROGRESSIVE PIANO STYLES

Jazz Improvisation III

John Mehegan

Watson-Guptill Publications/New York

Amsco Publications
New York/London/Sydney

In memory of my father, John James
and my mother, Margaret Louise Mehegan

CONTENTS

Preface by Horace Silver   7

Introduction   9

SECTION I   TEDDY WILSON

1. Scale-tone Tenths—"The Best Thing For You Is Me," in C   15
2. Major Scale-tone Tenth Inversions—"Lover Come Back To Me," in G   20
3. Dominant Scale-tone Tenth Inversions—"Autumn Leaves," in F   23
4. Minor Scale-tone Tenth Inversions—"The Song Is You," in D   25
5. Half-diminished Scale-tone Tenth Inversions—"Over The Rainbow," in Bb   28
6. Diminished Scale-tone Tenths—"Flying Down To Rio," in A   29
7. Major Swing Chords—"A Foggy Day," in Eb   31
8. Dominant Swing Chords—"Old Devil Moon," in E   33
9. Minor Swing Chords—"Cheek To Cheek," in Ab   35
10. Half-diminished Swing Chords—"Love For Sale," in B minor   37
11. Diminished Swing Chords—"I've Got My Love To Keep Me Warm," in Db   38
12. Chromatic Minor Tenths—"With A Song In My Heart," in Gb   40
13. Mixed Elements—"Thou Swell," in C   42
14. Integrated Hands—"What Is This Thing Called Love?" in G   44
15. Patterns (V-I)—"Gypsy In My Soul," in F   46
16. Right Hand Line—"My Heart Stood Still," in D   51

SECTION II   ART TATUM

17. Scale-tone Tenth Chords—"What's New?" in C   56
18. Sixty Scale-tone Tenth Chords—"You Do Something To Me," in G   59
19. Scale-tone Tenth Chord Inversions—"As Long As There's Music," in G   61
20. Mixed Positions (voicing)—"Time After Time," in D   64
21. Mixed Positions —Scale—Arpeggio Factors—Left Hand— "That Old Black Magic," in Bb   70
22. Mixed Positions (Axis of 7 and 3)—"Darn That Dream," in A   76
23. Mixed Positions, 3-7-3 (Major 3rd, Minor 7th) xxx cycle— "Prelude To A Kiss," in Eb   79
24. Mixed Positions, 7-3-7 (Minor 7th, Major 3rd) m-x-m cycle— "Satin Doll," in E   84
25. Mixed Positions, 7-3-7 (Minor 7th, Major 3rd) φ-x-φ cycle— "Woodyn' You," in Ab   88
26. Swing Bass—"April In Paris," in C   89
27. Pedaling—"Imagination," in C   92
28. Intros—"Stella By Starlight," in G   93

29. Melody—"Can't We Be Friends," in B♭ ... 97
30. The Harlem School—"Smoke Gets In Your Eyes," in D ... 99
31. Thomas "Fats" Waller—"Everything Happens To Me," in E♭ ... 101
32. Earl Hines—Traditional 12-bar blues, in A ... 103
33. Right Hand Components—"How About You?" in A♭ ... 105
34. "Walking" Bass Lines—"I've Got A Crush On You," in E ... 107
35. Classical Form-Jazz Content—"I've Gotta Right To Sing The Blues," in D♭ ... 109

SECTION III   BUD POWELL
36. Harmonic Fragmentation—Perfect Cycles—"Somebody Loves Me," in C ... 112
37. Harmonic Fragmentation—Diatonic—"Skylark," in G ... 114
38. Harmonic Fragmentation—Chromatic—"Memories Of You," in F ... 116
39. Alternate Cycles—"I Can't Get Started," in D ... 117
40. Right Hand Components (ballad)—"Angel Eyes," in G minor ... 120
41. Right Hand Components—(up tempo)—"Indiana," in A ... 122
42. Bass Lines—"Early Autumn," in E♭ ... 123
43. Building a Bass Line—"You Go To My Head," in A♭ ... 125

SECTION IV   GEORGE SHEARING
44. Block Chords—"I Got Rhythm," in 12 keys ... 128
45. The Five Qualities ... 130
46. The Melodic Points ... 143
47. The Chromatic Melodic Points ... 149
48. Solo Block Chords—"The Nearness Of You," in F ... 152
49. Block Chord Inversions—"Flamingo," in E♭ ... 156
50. Minor Scale-tone Block Chords—"Lullaby Of The Leaves," in C minor ... 158
51. Right Hand Block Chords—"Stardust," in D♭ ... 160
52. Block Chords with Left Hand Walking Line—"September In The Rain," in E♭ ... 162
53. Improvised Block Chords—"Don't You Know I Care," in E♭ ... 164

SECTION V   HORACE SILVER
54. General—"Falling In Love With Love," in E♭ ... 168
55. Technique—"One For The Road," in E♭ ... 169
56. Architecture—"The Breeze And I," in D ... 172
57. The Blues Tradition ... 173

PREFACE

In my opinion, the young aspiring musician has a difficult time of it trying to find good teachers and textbooks. This applies especially to the aspiring jazz musician.

In my youth I was plagued by many inadequate teachers who taught me incorrectly. This necessitated my being taught over again, not once, but several times. I fruitlessly searched the music stores for textbooks that would give me some knowledge of modern harmony as well as a beginner's approach to jazz improvisation.

In this book and in his two previous volumes, John Mehegan brings to the aspiring jazz musician a helping hand that will put the reader on the right track. May there be many more volumes to come.

Horace Silver

INTRODUCTION

The vast history of keyboard improvisation in America is a fantastic chronicle of human endeavor in confronting one of the most complex "musical mechanisms" ever created by man — the piano.

This chronicle begins in the last decade of the nineteenth century and prevails today some sixty years later with many different forms and skills, but with the same desire to capture some fragment of beauty from the piano. Ossip Gabrilowitsch, the renowned classical improvisor of the early twentieth century, once commented that no man could hope to subdue the piano, but he added, that if it is approached with great affection and humility, it sometimes gives back small moments of truth.

This quest for *beauty* and *truth* has taken many forms dictated by the technical levels existing in a culture; the demands of the social arena which the music reflects; the more repressive demands of the marketplace where the music must be sold; and, finally, the prevailing media of communication through which the music is presented to the audience. Media, in this case, would be a generic term which would include brothels, saloons, bars, dance halls, piano rolls, records, concerts, and sheet music. From and through these various media, piano improvisation has created a world of sound, of which this volume will deal with a part — namely, jazz piano from 1935 to 1950

Why jazz piano? And why 1935 to 1950? Firstly, jazz piano because it was and is the jazz pianist who has been the creator, forging new ideas, which in turn are adapted by more clever and less talented people for their own purposes. Secondly, 1935 to 1950 (Volume IV will deal with jazz piano from 1950 to the present day) represents a culmination of the ragtime tradition dating back to 1900; it also represents the years in which this great tradition was destroyed and replaced by the modern innovations of the "bop" era

In referring at the beginning of this introduction to "keyboard improvisation," it is understood that the term "improvisation" includes a vast assemblage of non-classical styles and attitudes of which jazz is only a segment. From this quarter, never the less, jazz is the segment most worthy of detailed and serious description, since it was and is the creative font of the entire field.

It might be interesting to arrange an outline of the history of non-classical piano improvisation in America in order to give the reader a frame of reference about this vast subject. The following breakdown of periods and styles is only schematic and does not by any means entirely encompass the field.

1900 - 1920

      RAGTIME

            Scott Joplin
            James Scott
            Tom Turpin
            Charles Lamb
            James P. Johnson
            Lucky Roberts

      MINSTREL-VAUDEVILLE

            Eubie Blake
            Buck Washington
            Jimmy Durante

      BARREL HOUSE

            Fate Marable
            Tony Jackson
            "Jelly Roll" Morton
            Rufus Perryman
            Porter King

      NOVELTY

            Zez Confrey
            Axel Christensen
            Felix Arndt

1920 - 1930

      BOOGIE-WOOGIE

            Jimmy Yancey
            "Pine-Top" Smith
            "Cow-Cow" Davenport
            Albert Ammons
            Pete Johnson
            Meade Lux Lewis

      JAZZ

            Willie "The Lion" Smith
            "Fats" Waller
            Earl Hines
            Elmer Schoebel
            Teddy Weatherford
            Arthur Schutt
            Joe Sullivan
            Art Hodes

POPULAR

Vincent Lopez
Pauline Alpert (The whirlwind pianist)
Ohman and Arden
Vee Lawnhurst
Joe Reichman
Roy Bargy
Ramona
George Gershwin

1930 - 1940

JAZZ

Art Tatum
Teddy Wilson
Mary Lou Williams
Count Basie
Jess Stacy
Claude Hopkins
Bob Zurke

POPULAR

Eddie Duchin
Henry King
Lee Sims
Maurice Rocco
Ray Noble
Lennie Hayton

1940 - 1950

JAZZ

Nat Cole
Bud Powell
George Wallington
Nat Jaffe
George Shearing
Horace Silver
Erroll Garner
Thelonious Monk
Lennie Tristano

POPULAR

Frankie Carle
Carmen Cavellero
Mel Powell
Jan August

1950 - 1962

JAZZ

Oscar Peterson
Hampton Hawes
Bill Evans

POPULAR

Andre Previn

Ahmad Jamal

Cy Walter

Peter Nero

Dave Brubeck

Don Shirley

Eddie Heywood

Skitch Henderson

NOVELTY

Joe "Fingers" Carr

Liberace

George Feyer

Jose Melis

Roger Williams

REVIVALIST

Dick Wellstood

Wally Rose

Don Ewell

Ralph Sutton

An interesting aspect of the period 1935 to 1950 has been a plethora of "method" books, each purporting to reveal the various resources employed by the pianists under consideration in this volume. None of these "methods" had any resemblance to the realities of the music they attempted to describe. Most of them concentrated on the swing-bass systems of Tatum and Wilson; the irony here lies in the fact, that all of these "method" books, without exception, employed inept ragtime mannerisms which were even impermissible in the ragtime era of the first two decades in this century, let alone in the swing era.

One of the most pernicious devices constantly employed by these methods was the "rolled" or broken tenth which no ragtime pianist ever employed. The reason for this was apparent, since few people could hope to encompass the hand span demands of an authentic swing-bass system this side of surgery.

A second major defect of these methods was the primitive harmonic grammar which could not possibly portray the vastness of the swing-bass systems. As we will learn in the first section of this volume, one minor tenth can be the bass structure for some eight harmonic functions; e.g. a G minor tenth is capable of supporting the following functions:

$$\text{Gm, } \text{G}\phi, \text{ EbM } \tfrac{6}{5}, \text{ E}\phi \tfrac{6}{5}, \text{ Ebx } \tfrac{6}{5}, \text{ Cx } \tfrac{4}{3}, \text{ and Cm } \tfrac{4}{3}$$

A third defect which revealed the aesthetic poverty of these methods was the "melody-fill-melody-fill" device of connecting the melodic phrases of a tune with senseless "runs" and "fills" without regard for the self-impelled continuity of the improvised line.

The early "barrel-house" or "blues" pianists such as Tony Jackson and "Jelly Roll" Morton employed a complex system of octaves and sixths on beats one and three, and a swing chord on beats two and four. The rag pianists generally abandoned the major and minor sixths in the bass in favor of the octave which represented an *open* interval and as such reduced the diffuse sound of the sixth.

An important device of the rag pianists was the use of the "back" beat which represented an interruption of the "root-chord-root-chord" displacements; e.g. *root-chord-chord-root, root-root-chord-root*, etc. The speed with which the rag pianists could execute these rapid displacements was incredible; often the left hand would appear only as a blur since the eye could not possibly follow this fantastic speed. The pianist would deliberately refrain from watching the keyboard since, as any sleight of hand performer can illustrate, the hand is quicker than the eye.

The first recorded example of the use of the tenth was in 1921 by James P. Johnson in "Keep Off The Grass." Johnson was the teacher of "Fats" Waller who extended the swing-bass system by introducing the sustaining pedal as an important adjunct of the tenth-chord structure. By pedaling the swing-bass, Waller was able to create a thunderous beat which exuded all the vitality and joy so much a part of this giant pianist.

In the twenties a new style of swing-bass piano developed in Harlem, which became known as "Harlem" or "stride" piano. The term stride evolved from the use of a single note in the deep bass "striding" up to the swing chord. By using the single note, the stride pianists were able to achieve an even more incredible speed in their left-hand motion. Thus, the use of the single note permitted more freedom in the harmonic functions of the left-hand since only the extended fifth finger was necessary to strike the bass note reducing the "traveling" distance of the left-hand movement, particularly in striking the black keys. This advantage further allowed for more chromatic roots moving in more complex inverted chords than previously possible. An added asset of the single note root was an improved architectural relationship between the left and right hands by reducing the ponderous octave in the bass register. Waller and Willie "The Lion" Smith along with James P. Johnson were the great stride players of the twenties.

Wilson and Tatum utilized the innovations of the Harlem school which were particularly applicable to the left-hand structure. The right-hand idioms of the Harlem school were generally immersed in tiresome ragtime idioms which possessed none of the freedom to be found in the developed *horn line* of contemporary saxophone and trumpet players.

The new concepts in the right hand improvised line came from an entirely different source — Midwesterner Earl Hines. Hines, formerly a ragtime pianist, had seen the ragtime prison of the right hand and turned to the soaring melodic genius of Louis Armstrong to free the right hand from the oppressive mannerisms of ragtime.

Wilson was primarily concerned with form and architecture; Tatum with an incredible content of new ideas and feelings which were to pave the way for succeeding developments. Both Wilson and Tatum carried the evolution of swing-bass through probably a century of classical harmonic idioms only to hear the entire edifice topple before their ears under the smashing assault of Bud Powell, Nat Cole and Thelonious Monk.

The demise of swing-bass also spelled the end of solo piano as an exuberant and flourishing art. It would seem in armchair retrospect that solo jazz piano might have endured this transition by adapting new measures which could have insured the continuation of such a vital adjunct of jazz. The decision to reduce the role of jazz piano to a rhythm section component was made by Bud Powell, and we must assume his genius inexorably led him to this inevitable and true conclusion.

Actually, Powell did achieve a partial reconstruction of solo piano in such recordings as "Dusk in Sandi" and "Glass Enclosure," but, as this master pianist withdrew from active involvement in jazz, solo piano ceased to exist, since none of Powell's contemporaries, or the men who carried on his achievement, seriously pursued this aspect of the art form.

Nat Cole abandoned jazz for worlds in which no jazzman can hope to survive; Monk remained a figure of obscurity whose achievements are more philosophical than pianistic. Powell emerges as the master architect of the early bop movement, Shearing the master consolidator. Shearing's "blowing line" is out of Powell, his block chord system an act of his own personal genius abetted by such diverse personalities as Glenn Miller and the Impressionist composers.

Horace Silver is an innovator of content breathing new life and substance into already existing forms. He has spawned a "content" school of "funky" piano represented by such performers as Andre Previn, Russ Freeman, the late Eddie Costa, John Williams and a host of other pianists. He has also been a collateral influence on Hampton Hawes, Oscar Peterson, Les McCann and many others.

More important, Silver has infused new life and meaning into the substratum of the blues and gospel tradition. At a time when jazz seems rendered apart by the invasion of exotic idioms of other cultures, it appears imperative that jazzmen look to their own roots and past for fresh inspiration. Silver has achieved this and in so doing has enriched the art form and reaffirmed the peculiar essence of jazz which has always distinguished it from all other forms of musical expression known to contemporary man.

John Mehegan
New York City
March, 1964

Teddy Wilson

LESSON 1.

Scale-tone Tenths

The first organization of the scale-tone chords to be considered, is the swing-bass tenth system developed by Teddy Wilson to a high degree of contrapuntal perfection when joined with an improvised line in the right hand. A tenth is a displaced third (Fig. 1). Any tenth may be constructed simply by extracting the *two lower tones* of any scale-tone chord or any inversion, and displacing the top tone up one octave (Figs. 2 and 3).

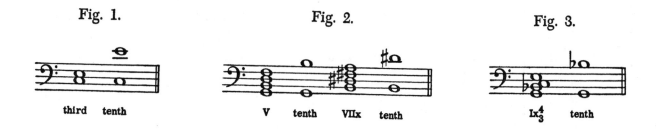

Fig. 1.   Fig. 2.   Fig. 3.

The essential features of this system are as follows:
1. Swing-bass tenths (Fig. 4)
2. Chromatic scale-tone tenths (Fig. 5)
3. Diatonic scale-tone tenths (Fig. 6)
4. Mixed elements (Fig. 7)

Fig. 4.

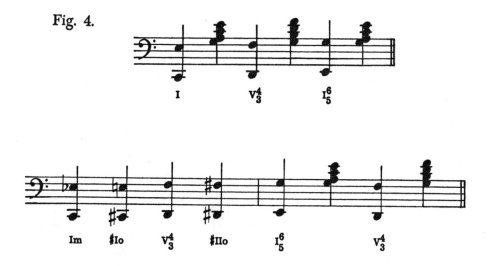

Fig. 6.

I   II   III   IV   V   IV   III   II   I

Fig. 7.

VIIx   III   bIII   II   bVIIo   II$^4_3$ V   IV   III   II   I

This system must be approached from both the *horizontal* (Figs. 5 and 6) and *vertical* (Fig. 4) points of view in order to capture its intrinsic beauty. To employ exclusively vertical swing-bass formulas (Fig. 4) in describing this system is to rob it of much of its contrapuntal elegance.

The primary device of Wilson's system is the scale-tone tenths played on the twelve major scales (Figs. 8-20).

Fig. 8.

I   II   III   IV   V   VI   VII   I

Fig. 9.

I   II   III   IV   V   VI   VII   I

Fig. 10.

I   II   III   IV   V   VI   VII   I

16

Fig. 11

Fig. 12.

Fig. 13.

Fig. 14.

Fig. 15.

Fig. 16.

Fig. 17.

Fig. 18.

I II III IV V VI VII I

Fig. 19.

I II III IV V VI VII I

Fig. 20.

I II III IV V VI VII I

Most students will find this entire system beyond their reach, since a basic eleven-note span is essential to perform every position (D♭ to F requires the widest span). "Breaking" the tenth is absolutely impermissible, since it disturbs the smoothness of the contrapuntal lines. In tenths beyond the student's reach, only the third (top voice) should be played.

On the basis of their span, tenths break down into the following categories:

Span 1:		Span 2:		Span 3:	
C — E♭		C — E		D♭ — F	
C♯ — E		D — F		D — F♯	
F — A♭		E♭ — G♭		E♭ — G	
F♯ — A		E — G		E — G♯	
G — B♭		F — A		A♭ — C	
{ G♯ — B }		G — B		A — C♯	
{ A♭ — C♭ }		A — C		B♭ — D	
		B♭ — D♭		B — D♯	
		B — D		{ G♭ — B♭ }	
				{ F♯ — A♯ }	

Spans 1 and 2 are within the reach of the average pianist; span 3, involving major tenths between black and white notes, in addition to G♭-B♭, is beyond the normal hand span. As a result, the material to be presented in this section will employ spans 1 and 2 only. Models of Wilson's bass lines taken from recordings will, of course, follow spans 1, 2, and 3 as played.

In accepting these practical limitations there is no doubt that some of the linear beauty of Wilson's system will be lost; however, the exclusion of span 3, will by no means represent a serious distortion of this magnificent style.

The techniques illustrated in the preceding Figs. 4, 5, 6, and 7 represent the basic tools employed by Wilson to connect two root position chords by long bass lines rich in harmonic implication. Because of the constant presence of these long contrapuntal lines, the harmonic system employed by Wilson is of a more complicated nature than that employed by contemporary pianists. The materials dealing with swing piano will be presented in terms of the rhythmic and harmonic concepts maintained in the late Thirties and early Forties, when this monumental system was created.

Fig. 21 is a base line for "The Best Thing For You" in the key of C major. Note modulation. Employing scaletone seventh chords in the left hand, improvise on this base line reviewing material studied in Vol. I of Jazz Improvisation.

Fig. 21.

(C) ♭Vm VIIx / ♭Vφ IVx / III ♭IIIx / II ♭IIx / I VI /
(C) II V / I II / III IVm / ♭Vm VIIx / ♭Vφ IVx / III ♭IIIx /
(C) II ♭IIx / I VI / II V / I^{+6} / VI // (A♭) I / IV / VII /
(A♭) ♭VIIx / VI / VI$_2$ // (C) II III / IV V / ♭Vm VIIx /
(C) ♭Vφ IVx / III ♭IIIx / II ♭IIx / I I$_2$ / VI VI$_2$ / ♭Vφ /
(C) IVm / VI$_4$ ♭IIIx / II ♭IIx / I^{+6} / I^{+6} //

THE BEST THING FOR YOU — Words and Music by Irving Berlin.
Copyright 1950 Irving Berlin
Used by permission of Irving Berlin Music Corporation,
1650 Broadway, New York 19, N. Y.

DRILL: Practice Figs. 8-20 ascending and descending, striving for smooth, uninterrupted lines. Play only the third (top voice) on tenths beyond the student's reach. A loose wrist stroke should accompany the playing of each tenth.

LESSON 2.

The Major Scale-tone Tenth Inversions

Since we are excluding span 3 from our work, we will be in immediate need of the tenth inversion system, so necessary to swing-bass playing. A tenth inversion is derived in the same manner as a tenth root — simply by extracting the *two lower tones* of any scale-tone chord inversion and displacing the top tone up one octave.

Fig. 1 illustrates the root and $\frac{6}{5}$ positions of the 12 major chords and the tenths derived from these positions.

Fig. 1.

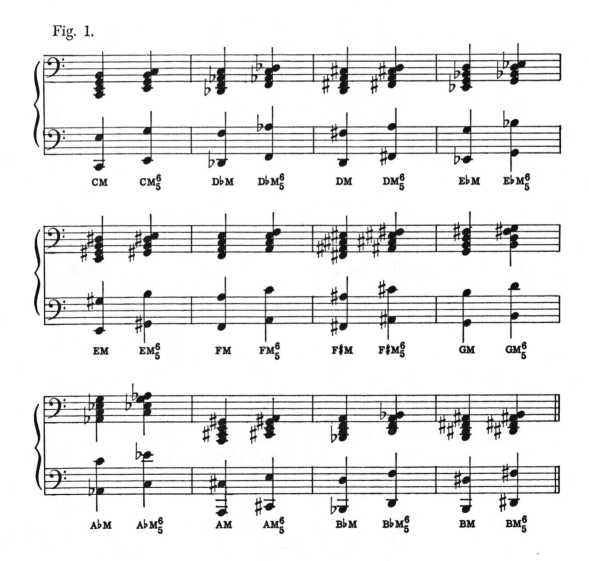

The major chord creates tenths in all root, $\frac{6}{5}$ and $\frac{4}{3}$ positions; the 2 position creates a ninth which is impractical in a swing-bass tenth system. Referring to Lesson 56, Volume I, the ninth appears in all five qualities and therefore carries no "qualifying" context; and is therefore excluded (Fig. 2). The major tenth on the $\frac{4}{3}$ position conveys a strong feeling of a root position major on V. To avoid this confusion between the major $\frac{4}{3}$ and the more compelling root position V, the major tenth on this position is omitted (Fig. 3).

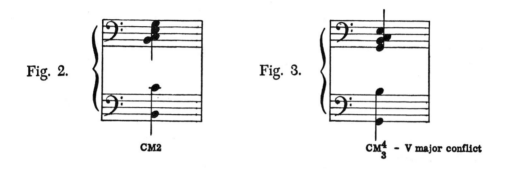

Fig. 2.   CM2

Fig. 3.   CM$\frac{4}{3}$ – V major conflict

Applying spans 1 and 2 to Fig. 1, we obtain the following tenth system for the 12 major chords (Fig. 4).

Fig. 4.

A$\flat$M$\frac{6}{5}$ CM   AM$\frac{6}{5}$ B$\flat$M$\frac{6}{5}$ BM$\frac{6}{5}$ CM$\frac{6}{5}$ FM   D$\flat$M$\frac{6}{5}$

DM$\frac{6}{5}$ E$\flat$M$\frac{6}{5}$ GM   EM$\frac{6}{5}$ FM$\frac{6}{5}$ F$\sharp$M$\frac{6}{5}$ GM$\frac{6}{5}$ CM

This offers a tenth system for all major chords enumerated in the following table:

root	6 5	4 3	2
C	D♭		
F	D		
G	E♭		
	E		
	F♯		
	A♭		
	A		
	B♭		
	B		

It must be kept in mind that spans 1 and 2 offer 15 tenths, which must perform the task of supporting a 204 chord harmonic system; as a result, each tenth must offer a number of "inferences," each of which is a harmonic fragment to be completed by the right hand improvisation.

DRILL: Practice the tenths in Fig. 4 for automatic facility with the 12 major chords.

Fig. 5 is a bass line for "Lover Come Back To Me" in the key of G. The sheet music of this tune appears in cut time (¢), thus the value of each melodic tone must be doubled in order to establish the correct meter for jazz.

Thus:

♪ becomes ♩

♩ becomes o

♩ becomes ♩

Fig. 5.

I $^{+6}$ / I / VII / ♭VIIx / VI / VI $_2$ / ♭Vφ / IVm / III / VI /

IIx $^{♭5}$ / V / I VI / ♭Vφ IVm / VI $_4$ $_3$ ♭IIIo / II ♭IIx / I $^{+6}$ / I /

VII / ♭VIIx / VI / VI $_2$ / ♭Vφ / IVm / III / VI / IIx $^{♭5}$ / V /

I VI / II ♭IIM / I $^{+6}$ IV / VII IIIx / VI $^{+6}$ / ♭Vφ /

VII IIIx $^{♯3}$ / VI $^{+6}$ ♭Vφ / VIIm / IIIx / IVx / IIIx / VI $^{+6}$ /

♭Vφ / VII IIIx $^{♯3}$ / VI / IIx / VI IIx / II / V / I $^{+6}$ /

I / VII / ♭VIIx / VI $^{♯7}$ / VI / IIIφ / ♭IIIx / II $^{♯♯7}$ II $^{♯7}$ / II /

VI $_2$ VI / II ♭IIx / I $^{+6}$ VI / II ♭IIM / I $^{+6}$ / I $^{+6}$ //

The Dominant Scale-tone Tenth Inversions

Fig. 1 illustrates the root, $\frac{6}{5}$ and $\frac{4}{3}$ positions of the twelve dominant chords with accompanying tenths; the $_2$ position which forms a ninth has been omitted.

Applying spans 1 and 2 to Fig. 1, we obtain the following: C, F, and G root positions and all $\frac{6}{5}$ and $\frac{4}{3}$ positions.

Fig. 1.

Fig. 2 illustrates the 27 possible positions for the dominant chord.

Fig. 2.

DRILL: Practice Fig. 2 for automatic facility with the dominant tenth positions.

The following table lists all possible dominant tenth positions:

root	6 5	4 3	2
C	C	C	
	Db	Db	
	D	D	
	Eb	Eb	
	E	E	
F	F	F	
	F#	F#	
G	G	G	
	Ab	Ab	
	A	A	
	Bb	Bb	
	B	B	

Fig. 3 is a base line for "Autumn Leaves" in E minor. Like "Lover Come Back To Me," "Autumn Leaves" appears in cut time (¢). The value of each melodic tone must be doubled in order to achieve the correct jazz meter.

Thus:

♪ becomes ♩
♩ becomes 𝅝
♩ becomes ♩
♩. becomes 𝅝♩
♩. becomes ♩.

Fig. 3.   pick-up

VI // II / V / I / IV / VII / IIIx / VI #7 / VI /

II / V / I / IV / VII / IIIx / VI +6 / VI +6 / IIIx / ♯Vo /

VI #7 / VI / II / V / I / IV / VII / IIIx / VI / ♭Vø /

VII / IIIx / VI +6 / VI +6 //

AUTUMN LEAVES — English Lyrics by Johnny Mercer, French Lyrics by Jacques Prevert, Music by Joseph Kosma, Copyright 1947 and 1950 by Enoch et Cie, published by Ardmore Music Corporation, New York and Hollywood, California. Used by permission.

"Autumn Leaves" is technically a "minor" tune, since it begins and ends on a minor chord; however, the *harmonic elements* employed are obviously major in character. Only the final cadence (last 6 bars) represents an authentic minor quality.

LESSON 4.

The Minor Scale-tone Tenth Inversions

Fig. 1 illustrates the root and $\frac{4}{3}$ positions of the twelve minor chords with accompanying tenths. The $\frac{6}{5}$ position has been omitted because of the major third formed by this inversion similar to the harmonic confusion described in relation to the $\frac{4}{3}$ position in Lesson 2. The $_2$ position has been omitted because of the impractical ninth formed. (See Lesson 2, Fig. 2).

Fig. 1.

Cm   Cm$\frac{4}{3}$ C♯m   C♯m$\frac{4}{3}$ Dm   Dm$\frac{4}{3}$ E♭m   E♭m$\frac{4}{3}$ Em   Em$\frac{4}{3}$ Fm   Fm$\frac{4}{3}$

Fig. 2 illustrates the 24 minor tenth positions.

Fig. 2.

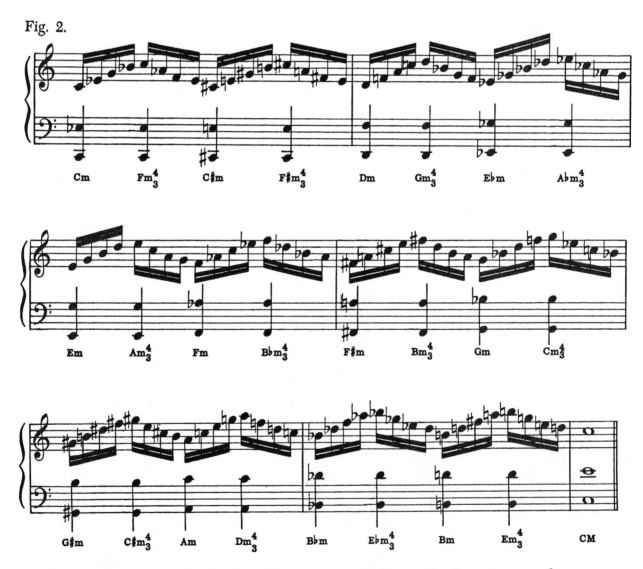

DRILL: Practice Fig. 2 for automatic facility with the minor tenth positions.

The following table lists all possible minor tenth positions:

root	6 5	4 3	2
C		C	
C#		C#	
D		D	
E♭		E♭	
E		E	
F		F	
F#		F#	
G		G	
G#		G#	
A		A	
B♭		B♭	
B		B	

Fig. 3 is a bass line for "The Song Is You" in the key of D major. Note modulations. Like the two previous songs, the following bass line is conceived in $\frac{4}{4}$ time, or $\frac{2}{4}$ double time (one bar becomes two, by doubling all the melodic values) which is usually associated with this tune in a jazz performance. Thus, a 32 bar tune is transformed into a 64 bar format.

Thus:

Fig. 3.

(D) VI$_{4 \atop 3}$ / ♭IIIo / II / V / I^{+6} / #Io / II / IVo / III / VI /

(D) II / V / IVm / ♭VIIx / III VI / II IVo / VI$_{4 \atop 3}$ / ♭IIIo /

(D) II / V / I^{+6} / #Io / II / IVo / III / ♭IIIx / II / ♭IIx /

(D) I^{+6} / VI // (F#) IIϕ / ♭IIx / I / VI / II / ♭IIx / I^{+6} /

(F#) I / ♭Vϕ / IVx / III$^{##7}$ / III$^{#7}$ / III / VIx / VI / IIx /

(F#) II / V // (D) VI$_{4 \atop 3}$ / ♭IIIo / II / V / I VI / Vm ♭V /

(D) IV / IVm / III / ♭IIIx / II / ♭IIx / I^{+6} VI / II V$^{#3}$ /

(D) I^{+6} / I^{+6} //

The Half-diminished Scale-tone Tenth Inversions

Fig. 1 illustrates the root and $\frac{6}{5}$ position of the twelve half-diminished chords with accompanying tenths. The $\frac{4}{3}$ position has been omitted because of the inaccessible major third (span 3). The $_2$ position has been omitted for the reason stated in the preceding chapters.

Fig. 1.

Fig. 2 illustrates the 24 half-diminished tenth positions.

Fig. 2.

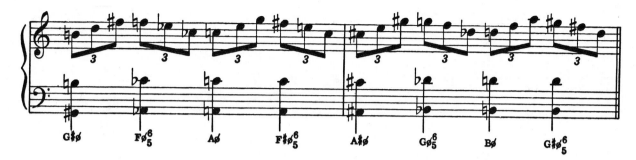

The following table lists all possible half-diminished tenth positions:

root		6 5	4 3	2
C		C		
C#		C#		
D		D		
D#		D#		
E		E		
F		F		
F#		F#		
G		G		
G#		G#		
A		A		
A#		A#		
B		B		

DRILL: Practice Fig. 2 for automatic facility with the half-diminished tenth positions.

Fig. 3 is a bass line for "Over The Rainbow" in the key of Bb major.

Fig. 3.

I $+^6$ bVϕ IVx / III VI / IV VII / III VI / II IVm / III bIIIx /

II bIIx / I $+^6$ #I / I $+^6$ bVϕ IVx / III VI / IV VII / III VI /

II IVm / III bIIIx / II bIIx / I $+^6$ #I / I VI / II VII$_4^3$ / III bIIIx /

II bIIx / I VI / bVϕ VIIx / III bIIIo / II V#^{3} / I $+^6$ bVϕ IVx /

III VI / IV VII / III VI / II IVm / III bIIIx / II bIIx / I $+^6$ //

OVER THE RAINBOW — Lyric by E. Y. Harburg — Music by Harold Arlen
© Copyright 1939 Leo Feist Inc., New York, N. Y.
Used by permission.

LESSON 6.

The Diminished Scale-tone Tenths

Since, in Volume I, we learned that the diminished chord cannot be inverted, it is therefore only necessary to illustrate the twelve root positions. Fig. 1 illustrates the 12 diminished chords with their accompanying tenths.

Fig. 1.

Fig. 2 illustrates the 12 diminished tenth positions.

Fig. 2.

The following table lists all possible diminished tenth positions:

root
C
C♯
D
E♭
E
F
F♯
G
G♯
A
B♭
B

DRILL: Practice Fig. 2 for automatic facility with the 12 diminished
tenths.

Fig. 3 is a bass line for "Flying Down To Rio" in A. Note the key change.

Fig. 3.

(A) I / II / III / IV / VI $_2$ / VI / II II $_2$ / VII $\flat$VIIx / VI $^{+6}$ /

(A) $\flat$Vϕ / VII / IIIx / IIIϕ / $\flat$IIIx / II / $\flat$IIx / I / II / III /

(A) IV / VI $_2$ / $\flat$V / IV / $\flat$VIIx / I // (F) II V / I VI /

(F) II $\flat$IIx / I VI // (A) III VI / IIx / $\flat$IIx / I / II / III /

(A) VI / II / $\flat$IIx / I $^{+6}$ / I $^{+6}$ //

LESSON 7.

The Major Swing Chords

As indicated in Lesson 1, an essential design of swing piano is the swing-bass technique which usually consists of a tenth played on the first and third beat followed by a "swing" chord on the second and fourth beat.

Technically this involves the problem of a rapid weight displacement, extending sometimes as far as three octaves.

Each swing chord is built upon a fairly fixed set of tones determined by the best arrangement of the elements each chord quality offers.

1. The first problem is one of register. Fig. 1 illustrates the normal limits of the "middle" area of the keyboard most suitable to create the tonal resonance of these chords.

Fig. 1.

2. The second consideration is one of finding the strongest arrangement of tones within the register illustrated in Fig. 1. Of the scale-tone chord inversions, (Fig. 2), the strongest position of the M, x, m, and φ qualities is the ₂ position (third inversion).

Fig. 2.

CM2   Cx2   Cm2   Cφ2

3. The final consideration is one of finding a chord voicing, with the most colorful top voice (the most obvious tone in any tonal combination). In this area there can be no doubt as to the overwhelming color of the third. (The fifth is not a color tone; the seventh, although a strong color tone, does not equal the third.)

From these three factors emerge the following tonal combination for the major chords based in each case upon the prevailing mode (Ionian) of the chord.

M — 5 6 1 3

This tonal combination is VI₂ (third inversion of the VI chord in the prevailing key). Wilson's harmonic system usually excluded the major seventh either in root position or any of its inversions; the ₂ position of the minor VI chord fulfills the usual added sixth treatment of the major I chord.

Following a C major tenth, this would mean playing G A C É — 5 6 1 3 based on the Ionian mode of C. All tenth inversions studied in Lessons 2 through 5, take the same chord as the root position tenth.

Applying the major tenths of spans 1 and 2 illustrated in Fig. 4, Lesson 2, to the 5 6 1 3 combination, we derive the following:

Fig. 3.

CM   CM⁶₅   DbM⁶₅   DM⁶₅   EbM⁶₅

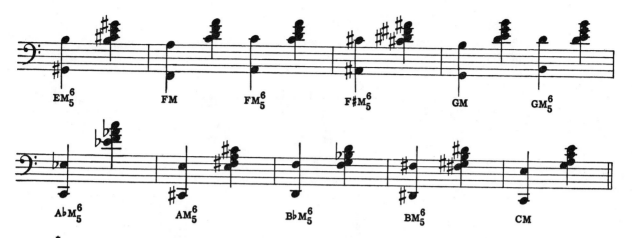

Fig. 4 is a bass line for "A Foggy Day" in E♭.

Fig. 4.

pick-up

♭IIx // I / IIIϕ ♭IIIx / II / ♭IIx / I⁺⁶ / VIϕ IIx♯⁵ / II / V♯³ /

I VI / Vm ♭V / IV / IVm ♭VIIx / III / ♭IIIx / II / V♯³ / I /

IIIϕ ♭IIIx / II / ♭IIx / I⁺⁶ / VIϕ IIx♯⁵ / II / V / Vm / ♭V / IV /

♭VIIx / I VII / VI Vm / IV VI₄ / II ♭IIx / I⁺⁶ / I⁺⁶ //
$\qquad\qquad\qquad\qquad\qquad\quad$ 3

A FOGGY DAY —

DRILL: Practice Fig. 3 for automatic facility with the twelve major tenths (or their indicated inversions) and their swing chords. (The problem of weight displacement involves several factors: 1. Free, pendulum-like arm movement; 2. Loose wrist; 3. True facility which can only result from completely "blind" automation (Remember, the hand moves faster than the eye.)

LESSON 8.

The Dominant Swing Chords

The tonal combination for all dominant swing chords is 5 7 1 3 based on the Mixolydian mode of each dominant chord. All inversion tenths take the same chord.

Fig. 1 illustrates the dominant tenths appearing in Fig. 2, Lesson 3. The tonal combination 5 7 1 3 represents the $\frac{4}{3}$ inversion of the scale-tone dominant.

Fig. 1.

The A, B♭, and B dominant swing chords in Fig. 1 are technically and musically awkward, so are the same chords played one octave higher. To avoid these awkward positions, Wilson usually used a substitute voicing on these three dominants. These substitute voicings are built on the tonal combinations 7 1 3 5 (the third inversion of the scale-tone dominant). See Fig. 2.

Fig. 2.

DRILL: Practice Figs. 1 and 2 for automatic facility with the dominant swing chords.

Fig. 3 is a bass line for "Old Devil Moon" in the key of E. Note the key changes.

Fig. 3.

(E) I⁺⁶ / Vm / I⁺⁶ / Vm / I / Vm / I VI / Vm ♭V / IV /

(E) IV / IVm / ♭VIIx // (F) II ♭IIx / I⁺⁶ (E) ♭IIx / I⁺⁶ /

(E) I⁺⁶ Vm / I⁺⁶ / Vm // (D♭) I / I⁺⁶ // (E) VI / IIx /

(E) II / V#³ / I⁺⁶ / Vm / I⁺⁶ / Vm / I / Vm / I VI / Vm ♭V /

(E) IV / IV / IVm / ♭VIIx // (F) II ♭IIx / I⁺⁶ (E) ♭IIx / I⁺⁶ /

(E) I⁺⁶ Vm / I⁺⁶ / I⁺⁶ Vm / I⁺⁶ / IVm / IIIx ♭IIIx / II ♭IIx /

(E) I⁺⁶ / I⁺⁶ //

LESSON 9.

The Minor Swing Chords

The tonal combination for all minor swing chords is 7 1 3 5 based on the Dorian mode of each minor chord. All inversion tenths take the same chord.

This is the identical voicing employed in Lesson 7, although the relationship to the accompanying tenth is not the same. The tonal combination 7 1 3 5 represents the third inversion (²) of the scale-tone chord. Fig. 1 illustrates the minor tenths appearing in Fig. 2, Lesson 4, with their accompanying swing chords.

Fig. 1.

DRILL: Practice Fig. 1 for automatic facility with the minor tenths and their appropriate swing chords.

Fig. 2 is a bass line for "Cheek To Cheek" in A♭.

Fig. 2.

I $^{+6}$ ♯Io / II ♭IIx / I $^{+6}$ ♯Io / II ♭IIx / I $^{+6}$ VII $_{\substack{6 \\ 5}}$ / ♯IIo III /

VIIm IIIx / VIx IIx / V IV / III II / ♭VIIx $^{♭5}$ / VIx / II / ♭IIx /

I $^{+6}$ VI / II ♭IIx / I $^{+6}$ ♯Io / II ♭IIx / I $^{+6}$ ♯Io / II ♭IIx /

I $^{+6}$ VII $_{\substack{6 \\ 5}}$ / ♯IIo III / VIIm IIIx / VIx IIx / V IV / III II /

♭VIIx $^{♭5}$ / VIx / II / ♭IIx / I $^{+6}$ / ♯Io / II IVo / VI $_4$ ♭IIIx / II ♭IIx /

I $^{+6}$ VI / II IVo / VI $_4$ ♭IIIx / II ♭IIx / I VI / II IVo / VI $_4$ ♭IIIx /

II ♭IIx / I $^{+6}$ VI / II IVo / VI $_4$ ♭IIIx / II ♭IIx / I $^{+6}$ / Im $^{♯♯7}$ Im $^{♯7}$ /

Im Im $_2$ / ♭III / ♭VIx / II / IVo / VI $_4$ ♭IIIx / II ♭IIx / I $^{+6}$ ♯Io /

II ♭IIx / I $^{+6}$ ♯Io / II ♭IIx / I $^{+6}$ VII $_{\substack{6 \\ 5}}$ / ♯IIo III / VIIm IIIx /

VIx IIx / V IV / III II / ♭VIIx $^{♭5}$ / VIx / II / ♭IIx / I $^{+6}$ / I $^{+6}$ //

LESSON 10.

The Half-diminished Swing Chords

The tonal combination for all half-diminished swing chords is 7 1 3 5 based on the Locrian mode of each half-diminished chord. All inversion tenths take the same chords.

The tonal combination 7 1 3 5 represents the third inversion ($_2$) of the scale-tone chord. Fig. 1 illustrates the half-diminished tenths appearing in Fig. 2, Lesson 5, with their accompanying swing chords.

Fig. 1.

DRILL: Practice Fig. 1 for automatic facility with the half-diminished tenths and their appropriate swing chords.

Fig. 2 is a bass line for "Love For Sale" in B. This song defies the normal conventions of cadencing by moving arbitrarily between a major and minor tonality. It is usually considered a "minor" tune although it begins and ends on basic major harmonic elements.

Fig. 2.

(B)   IV / IV^{+6} / Im$^{\sharp 7}$ / Im / IV / IV^{+6} / Im$^{\sharp 7}$ / Im / IV //

(D)   II ♭IIx / I // (C) II V // (b) II / ♭IIx / Im / Im^{+6} //

(B)   IV / IV^{+6} / I / I^{+6} / IV / IV^{+6} / I / I^{+6} / IV //

(D)   II ♭IIx / I^{+6} // (C) II V // (b) II / ♭IIx / Im / Im^{+6} //

(D)   II / ♭IIx / I II / III ♭IIIx / II / ♭IIx / I II / III IV /

(D)   III VIx / ♭VIIx VIx / II$^{\sharp\sharp 7}$ II$^{\sharp 7}$ / II // (B) VIϕ IIx /

(B)   VIϕ IIx / ♭VI ♭IIx / Vϕ Ix / IV / IV^{+6} / Im$^{\sharp 7}$ / Im /

(B)   IV / IV^{+6} / I / I^{+6} / IV // (D) II ♭IIx / I^{+6} // (C) II V //

(b)   II / ♭IIx / Im / Im$_2$ / VI / VI$_2$ / IV VI$_4$ / II ♭IIx //
                                                          $_3$

(B)   ♭Vϕ IVm / VI$_4$ Iϕ$_6$ / II ♭IIM / I^{+6} //
                   $_3$ $_5$

LESSON 11.

The Diminished Swing Chords

Since the diminished chord has no context in any tonality, the swing chord is determined on the basis of register and its relation to the prevailing diminished series determined by the tenth.

We learned in Volume I, that there are twelve diminished chords falling into three series:

1. Co - E♭o - G♭o - Ao

2. C♯o - Eo - Go - B♭o

3. Do - Fo - A♭o - Bo

This means that *the members of any particular series may be used with any diminished tenth belonging to that series.* This does not mean that the tenths of any series can be interchanged, only the swing chords appearing over the tenths.

Fig. 1 illustrates the twelve diminished tenths with their appropriate swing chords (note third is top voice). To avoid the awkward positions of the Ao, B♭o, and Bo swing chords, the next chord in the series is often employed as in Fig. 2.

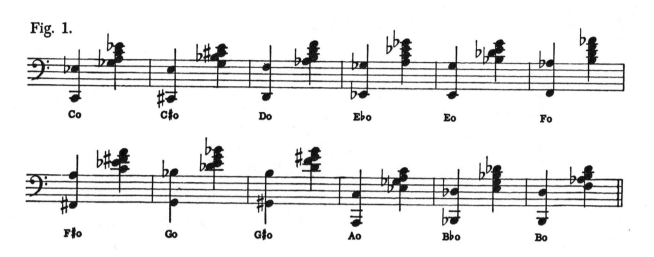

This in no way affects the basic value of the structure, which is determined by the root of the tenth — nothing else. Thus, in Fig. 3, the four swing chords illustrated are all part of a Co series.

DRILL: Practice Fig. 1 for automatic facility with the diminished tenths and their appropriate swing chords.

Fig. 3.

Fig. 4 is a bass line for "I've Got My Love To Keep Me Warm" in D♭.

Fig. 4.

pick-up

IVo // VI$_4$ / ♭IIIo / II / V / ♭Vø / VIIx / VIIx / ♭IIIo / II / ♭IIo /

II / ♭IIx $\overset{3}{/}$ I Ix$_2$ / II$_4$ ♭VIo / VI$_2$ ♭Vo / IV IVo / VI$_4$ / ♭IIIo / II /

V / ♭Vø / VIIx / VIIx $\overset{3}{/}$ ♭IIIo / II / ♭IIo / II / ♭IIx $\overset{3}{/}$ I VI /

II ♭IIx / I^{+6} VI / ♭Vø IVx / III$^{\#\#7}$ / III$^{\#7}$ / III / VIx / II$^{\#\#7}$ /

II$^{\#7}$ / II / V / VI$_4$ / ♭IIIo / II / V / ♭Vø / VIIx / VIIx / ♭IIIo /

II / ♭IIo / II / ♭IIx $\overset{3}{/}$ I VI / II ♭IIx / I^{+6} / I^{+6} //

LESSON 12.

The Chromatic Minor Tenths

In Volume I we learned that there are three basic harmonic patterns present in all jazz improvisation:

1. Circle of Fifths

2. Diatonic

3. Chromatic

1. The circle of fifths is, of course, a basic ingredient of all swing piano, but the prevalent use of inversions by Wilson (particularly in the dominant chord) reduces the value of this pattern, which can only be effective in the root position.

2. Diatonic patterns mean employing span 3, which has been ruled out for practical considerations, although in Wilson's playing they do constitute at least a pattern of some importance.

3. The use of chromatic patterns as connecting fragments is essential to Wilson's style and fortunately falls in spans 1 and 2 and is therefore within the average reach.

As a preparation for the use of these chromatic patterns, complete facility with the chromatic minor scale-tone tenths (Fig. 1) is essential. Since we have learned that each minor tenth must support more than one quality through the use of inversions, it should be clear to the student that the term "minor" applied to a tenth (displaced minor third) describes its architectural value on the keyboard, not the chord quality involved.

Fig. 1.

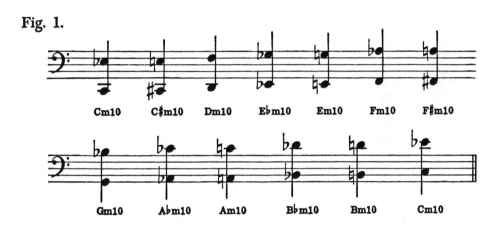

Cm10   C♯m10   Dm10   E♭m10   Em10   Fm10   F♯m10

Gm10   A♭m10   Am10   B♭m10   Bm10   Cm10

Fig. 2 is a bass line for "With A Song In My Heart" in G♭.

Fig. 2.

I VI / II ♭IIx / I IV / VII ♭VIIx / VI⁺⁶ ♭Vφ / VII ♭VIIx /

VI⁺⁶ ♭Vφ / VII ♭VIIx / VI VI₂ / ♭Vφ / IVx / ♭Vφ₂ / IVx₂ /

♭Vm IVx / III ♭IIIx / II ♭IIx / I VI / II ♭IIx / I IV / VII ♭VIIx /

VI⁺⁶ ♭Vφ / VII ♭VIIx / VI⁺⁶ ♭Vφ / VII ♭VIIx / VI / ♭VIx♭⁵ /

VI₂ / ♭Vφ IVm / VI₄ ♭IIIo / II ♭IIx / I⁺⁶ / I⁺⁶ //
              ₃

DRILL: Practice Fig. 1, ascending and descending, for automatic facility; employ a loose wrist and arm. On tenths employing a black note root (C♯, E♭, F♯, A♭, and B♭), the fourth finger and thumb is the preferable fingering. Use fifth finger and thumb on all remaining tenths. If 4-1 is beyond the student's reach, use 5-1 on all tenths.

Mixed Elements

In order to create an interesting *underpinning* for an improvisation, it is necessary to introduce many variables of the elements studied in Lessons 1 through 12. Fig. 1 illustrates some of these mixed elements in a swing-bass arrangement for "Thou Swell" in the key of C. These elements include:

1. Swing-bass (bars 1, 2)
2. Chromatic minor tenths (bars 3, 5, 6)
3. Diatonic tenths using spans 1 and 2 (bars 4, 15, 16)
4. A single bass note on the fifth of prevailing chord (bars 7, 17, 21)
5. Half-note tenths (bars 9, 18, 19, 22, 24, 25, 26)
6. Broken quarter-note tenths (bar 10)
7. Half note sevenths and thirds (bars 13, 14)
8. Whole-note sevenths (bar 27)
9. Mixed sevenths and tenths (bar 28)
10. Eighth-note syncopations (bar 32)

Fig. 1.

Fig. 2 represents a basic chord line for "Thou Swell."

Fig. 2.

pick-up

♯Io // II ♭IIo / II V / III ♭IIIx / II ♭IIx / I II / III IV /

Vm Ix / ♭V∅ VIIx / III VIx / II V / I / IV / VIIm ♭VIIx /

VI ♭VIx / V IV / III ♭IIIx / II ♭IIo / II V / III ♭IIIx / II ♭IIx /

I II / III IV / Vm Ix / ♭V∅ VIIx / III VIx / II V / ♭VIIx$^{♭\,5}$ /

VIx / IIx / II ♭IIx / I$^{+\,6}$ / I$^{+\,6}$ //

DRILL: Build a right-hand improvisation on Fig. 1, using Wilson's recorded solo in Volume II as a model. Note the following characteristic right-hand elements:

1. Eighth-note unit
2. Mixed single-note octave elements
3. Punctuation

The use of sevenths and thirds is fully discussed in Lesson 72 of Volume I

LESSON 14.

Integrated Hands

The swing-bass studies in Lessons 7 through 11 encompass more than two-thirds of the normal playing register of the piano.

Fig. 1: playing register   Fig. 2: swing-bass register

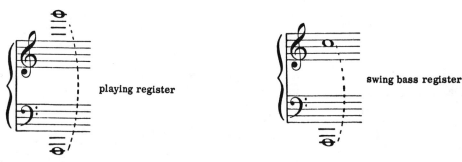

This space-consuming left-hand device seriously restricts the ability of the right hand to take full advantage of the richest registers of the keyboard.

Wilson's solution to this problem was an eminently simple one, namely, to hold half or whole-note tenths in the left hand, while moving the right hand down into the register usually reserved for the swing chords.

This is, of course, self-evident; what is not so self-evident is that Wilson's right-hand melodic continuity, as it moves from one register to another, determines the movement of the left hand. This concern with the melodic flow of the right-hand line, and the ability to integrate the left hand into the over-all concept, is the key to the magnificent contrapuntal beauty of the style. A basic rule seems to prevail, which is never to repeat the identical left-hand "set-up" in two consecutive bars.

Fig. 3 is a swing-bass improvisation for "What Is This Thing Called Love" in the key of C. When building a right-hand line, keep in mind the principle of integrated hands. Note the many key changes, including the deceptive opening fragment in F minor (*See Minor Scale-tone Chords, Volume I*). The key series for Fig. 3 is F minor, C major, F minor, C major, B♭ major, D♭ major (*unresolved*), C major (*unresolved*), F minor, and C major.

Fig. 3.

44

45

Fig. 4 is a chord bass line for "What Is This Thing Called Love."

Fig. 4.

pick-up

(f) ♯Ix // II / ♭IIx / I / Im₂ // (C) IIφ / ♭IIx / I / I // (f) II /

(f) ♭IIx / I / Im₂ // (C) IIφ / ♭IIx / I⁺⁶ / I⁺⁶ // (B♭) II /

(B♭) ♭IIx / I / I // (D♭) II / V // (C) II / V // (f) II /

(f) ♭IIx / I / Im₂ // (C) IIφ / ♭IIx / I⁺⁶ / I⁺⁶ //

LESSON 15.

Patterns (V-I)

Since by now we are familiar with the constant appearance in every tune of identical chord sequences (*patterns*), the importance of dealing with these patterns as a single automatic unit can hardly be overestimated. The basic fragment of all these patterns is V-1, which will be considered here in each of the 12 keys. In Fig. 1, key of C, the basic chord pattern appears in the lower figured bass; the temporary chordal elements passed through appear in the upper figured bass. These passing elements are, in a sense, the essence of the harmonic beauty of Wilson's style. The moving inflections create a chromatic mosaic imbuing a simple chord sequence with a kaleidoscope of color and imagery. The spelling of $V\frac{4}{3}$ on the fourth beat of bar 1 and the third beat of bar 2 is in keeping with Wilson's device of correctly treating the tenth on D as an inversion of V, since to move from II to I, bypassing V, is a weak harmonic progression.

Fig. 1.

Figs. 2-12 illustrate a variety of this basic pattern in 12 keys using spans 1 and 2 only.

Figs. 2-12.

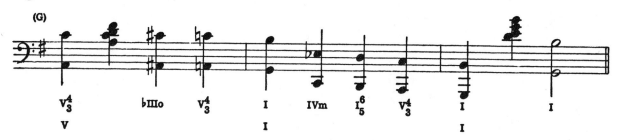

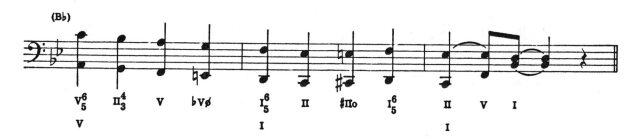

Fig. 13 is a swing bass for "Gypsy In My Soul" in F. Note the double bridge.

Fig. 13.

DRILL: Practice Figs. 2-12 for automatic facility with V-I patterns.

Fig. 14 is a bass line for "Gypsy In My Soul" in F.

Fig. 14.

I VI / II IVo / III VI / II V / I VI / ♭Vϕ IVo / VI₄ ♭IIIo /

II ♭IIx / I VI / II IVo / III VI / II V / I VI / II ♭IIx / I⁺⁶ II /

♯IIo VI₄ / III♯♯⁷ / III♯⁷ / III / VIx / II♯♯⁷ / II♯⁷ / II / V /

I VI / II IVo / III VI / II V / I VI / II ♭IIx / I⁺⁶ / ♭IIIo /

II / IVo / III / VI / ♭Vϕ / VIIx / III VIx / II V / I VI / II IVo /

III VI / II V / I VI / II ♭IIx / I⁺⁶ / I⁺⁶ //

LESSON 16.

Right Hand Line

A melody consists of a succession of intervals punctuated through by rest values. Why some melodies are memorable and others not is a question no textbook can completely answer. Why some improvisations are more "melodic" than others, is also a question not to be fully answered. In the case of Wilson, one of the most melodic of all jazzmen, the materials employed are so illusively simple as to deceive even the most thoroughly trained musician. As the transcription in Volume II, page 80 will indicate, the eighth-note is almost without exception the sole melodic unit. The eighth-note unit is, however, punctuated by a masterful use of rest values extending from the eighth-note rest to the double whole-note rest.

Using improvisation studies in Volume I, in addition to a careful study of the models in Volume II, build "blowing" lines, on the bass lines appearing in the previous lessons. When building these lines, keep the following ideas in mind:

RHYTHMIC:
1. A basic eighth-note unit.
2. A partial use of the quarter-note unit as well as the eighth-note triplet.
3. Eighth-note syncopation.
4. An extensive range of rest values from the eighth-note to double whole-note.

HARMONIC:
1. Arpeggio-oriented lines with occasional modal scale connecting fragments.
2. Sparse use of chromatic tones.

ARCHITECTURAL:
1. Single notes and octaves in an integrated line.
2. Occasional use of octave line.
3. Occasional use of inner harmonic voices added within the octave.

These studies are based upon the early period (1936-1940) of Wilson's playing and therefore will omit serious consideration of certain idiomatic "runs" associated with his more florid period (1940-1950). One of these idiomatic runs, made memorable by Wilson, is that built on the pentatonic (five-tone) scale, employed extensively in major, minor, and dominant chords, both ascending and descending, but more often descending.

Fig. 1 illustrates the fingering of these runs as used on the 12 major, dominant, and minor chords descending on degrees 1 6 5 3 2 1 of either the Ionian or Dorian modes of the prevailing chord. The Ionian mode also serves the dominant chord since the seventh of the chord is not involved.

Fig. 1.   Fingering:

C	M-x-m	4	(2	1	3	2	1	2	1	3	2	1)	etc.
Db	M-x-m	4	(3	2	1	2	1	3	2	1	2	1)	etc.
D	M-x-m	4	(2	1	3	2	1	2	1	3	2	1)	etc.
Eb	M-x-		(3	1	3	2	1	3	1	3	2	1)	etc.
	m		(3	1	4	2	1	3	1	4	2	1)	etc.
E	M-x-m	4	(2	1	3	2	1	2	1	3	2	1)	etc.
F	M-x-m	4	(2	1	3	2	1	2	1	3	2	1)	etc.
F♯	M-x-	4	(2	1	3	2	1	2	1	3	2	1)	etc.
	m	4	(3	2	1	2	1	3	2	1	2	1)	etc.
G	M-x-m	4	(2	1	3	2	1	2	1	3	2	1)	etc.
Ab	M-x-m	3	(1	3	1	3	2	1	3	1	3	2)	etc.
A	M-x-m	4	(2	1	3	2	1	2	1	3	2	1)	etc.
Bb	M-x-m		(3	2	1	2	1	3	2	1	2	1)	etc.
B	M-x-m	4	(2	1	3	2	1	2	1	3	2	1)	etc.

Extended runs employ repeated fingering, as marked within brackets.

Fig. 2 illustrates the pentatonic run on the major, dominant, and minor chords of C.

Fig. 2.

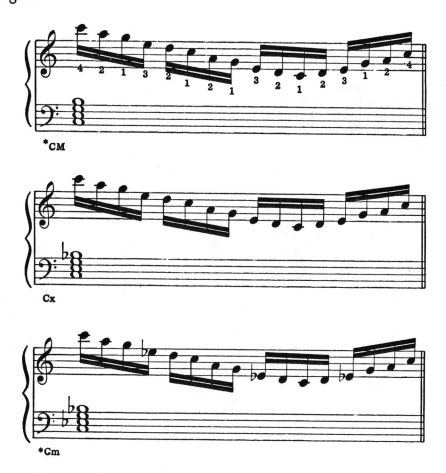

*CM

Cx

*Cm

* The pentatonic run may be played over the normal major, dominant or minor chords, or those with the added sixth (+6).

Fig. 3 is a swing bass for "My Heart Stood Still" in the key of D. Apply a right-hand improvisation to Fig. 3.

Fig. 4 is a bass line for "My Heart Stood Still." Note the key change.

Fig. 4.

(D) VI₄ ♭IIIo / II ♭IIx / I VI / IVm ♭VIIx / III VI / II V♯³ /

(D) III ♭IIIx / II V / VI₄ ♭IIIo / II ♭IIx / I VI / IVm ♭VIIx /

(D) III VI / II V♯³ / I / V♯³ // (A) IVm IVm♯⁷ / IVm₂ IIø / ♭IIx /

(A) I VI / IIø / V // (D) ♭III ♭VIx / II V / VI₄ ♭IIIo / II ♭IIx /

(D) I Ix / IV IVm / III ♭IIIo / II ♭IIx / I⁺⁶ / I⁺⁶ //

DRILL: Practice Fig. 1 for automatic facility with penatonic runs ascending and descending.

Art Tatum

LESSON 17.

The Scale-tone Tenth Chords

To approach the subject of Art Tatum's style is to be confronted with a fantastic universe of sound spanning some twenty years of pianistic rule. Here one finds a veritable maze of styles, idioms, and influences, in addition to a Picasso-like succession of periods, hardly achieved before abandoned. Ragtime, stride, swing, incipient bop, romanticism, impressionism, blues, and boogie woogie all appear in a turbulent maze of sound.

Tatum's Rabelaisian keyboard life can be divided into three main periods:

·1. Ragtime — "stride" period: 1930-1936.
2. Solo and swing period: 1936-1942.
3. Trio period: 1943-1957.

This study will concern itself with the *middle period* only. The *first period* is the amazing documentation of an emerging giant, although the performances were musically uneven, containing senseless virtuosity, often with little musical context.

The *third period* of Tatum's work is again a return to the same virtuosity which characterized the *first period,* but this time coupled with a breathtaking harmonic idiom, which too often pushed Tatum beyond the bounds of what can honestly be called "jazz."

It is in the *middle period* that Tatum's resources are joined in a perfect balance of swing, taste, invention, and, above all, simplicity; a severe editing of every last device, which was not always a natural inclination with this pianistic giant.

The cornerstone of Tatum's left hand lay in the scale-tone seventh chord, with the third displaced up an octave. Fig. 1 illustrates the scale-tone seventh chords of C; first, in normal closed position, then with the displaced third, forming scale-tone tenth chords.

Fig. 1.

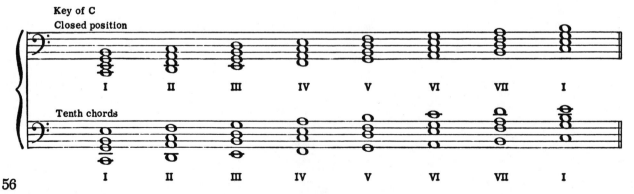

Figs. 2-12 illustrate the scale-tone tenth chords in the remaining keys. It is understood that the original chord qualities are still maintained. Thus, in all figures:

I is a MAJOR tenth
II is a MINOR tenth
III is a MINOR tenth
IV is a MAJOR tenth
V is a DOMINANT tenth
VI is a MINOR tenth
VII is a HALF-DIMINISHED tenth

Figs. 2-12.

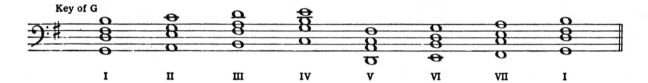

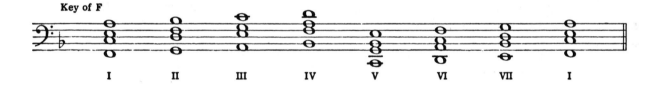

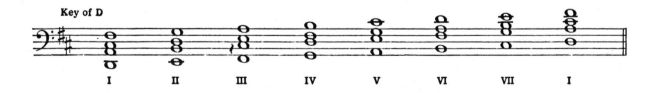

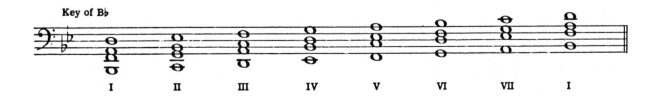

Key of A

I   II   III   IV   V   VI   VII   I

Key of E♭

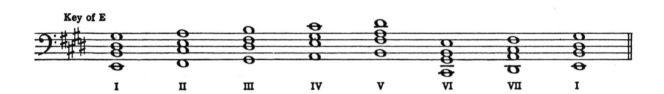

I   II   III   IV   V   VI   VII   I

Key of E

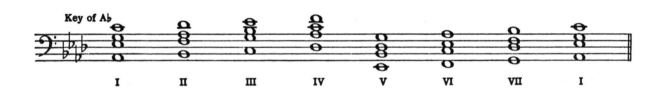

I   II   III   IV   V   VI   VII   I

Key of A♭

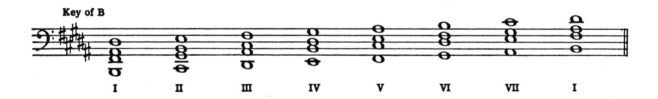

I   II   III   IV   V   VI   VII   I

Key of B

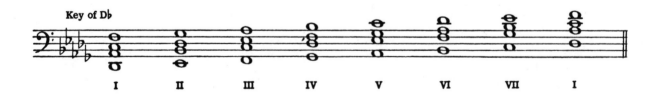

I   II   III   IV   V   VI   VII   I

Key of D♭

I   II   III   IV   V   VI   VII   I

Key of G♭

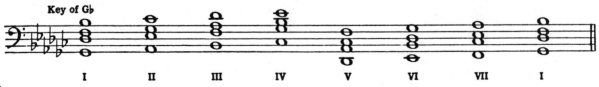

I   II   III   IV   V   VI   VII   I

Fig. 13 is a bass line for "What's New." Note the key changes from major to minor tonalities.

Fig. 13.

pick-up

(C) ♭IIx // I⁺⁶ VI // (A♭) II ♭IIx / I VI // (c) II ♭IIx /

(c) I VI / II ♭IIx // (C) I VI / II ♭IIx / I⁺⁶ VI // (A♭) II ♭IIx /

(A♭) I VI // (c) II ♭IIx / I VI / II ♭IIx // (C) I VI // (F) II ♭IIx /

(F) I⁺⁶ VI // (D♭) II ♭IIx / I VI // (f) II ♭IIx / I VI /

(f) II ♭IIx / I Im₂ // (C) IIϕ ♭IIx / I⁺⁶ VI // (A♭) II ♭IIx /

(A♭) I VI // (c) II ♭IIx / I VI / II ♭IIx // (C) I / I⁺⁶ //

DRILL: Play Figs. 1-12 with left hand when possible, or with both hands (root and fifth in the left) in instances of span difficulty. (See Lesson 69, Volume I.)

LESSON 18.

The Sixty Scale-tone Tenth Chords

Fig. 1 illustrates the sixty scale-tone tenth chords (M, x, m, ϕ, o) on twelve tones. As in Lesson 17, play these chords with both hands, or in the left hand, whenever the student's span allows.

Fig. 1.

Fig. 2 is a bass line for "You Do Something To Me" in the key of C.

Fig. 2

I^{+6} / Io / I^{+6} / ♭Vm $VIIx$ / I^{+6} VII_6 / ♯IIo VI_4 / IV ♯IVx / V /
(₅ under VII₆, ₃ under VI₄)

II / ♭IIo / II_2 / ♭$VIIx$ VIx / VI / IIx / II / V $IV\phi$ / I_6 / ♭$IIIo$ / VII_6 /
(₅ under I₆, ₅ under VII₆)

VIx_6 / IVm_4 / III_4 $III\phi_4$ / II_4 $II\phi_4$ / $V^{♯3}$ V / I^{+6} / ♭Vm $VIIx$ /
(₅ ₃ ₃ ₃ ₃ ₃ subscripts)

IVm ♭$VIIx$ / III VIx / ♭III ♭VIx / II ♭IIx / I^{+6} / I^{+6} //

DRILL: Practice Fig. 1 in the left hand whenever possible; root-fifth in
left hand, seventh-third in the right when playing tenths beyond
the student's span.

LESSON 19.

The Scale-tone Tenth Chord Inversions

Unlike Wilson, Tatum not only employed the full scale-tone tenth chords, but also the three inversion positions of each scale-tone chord (except the diminished chord, which is always in root position).

Fig. 1 illustrates the sixty scale-tone tenth chords and their inversions.

Fig. 1.

NOTE: Frames indicate span 3.

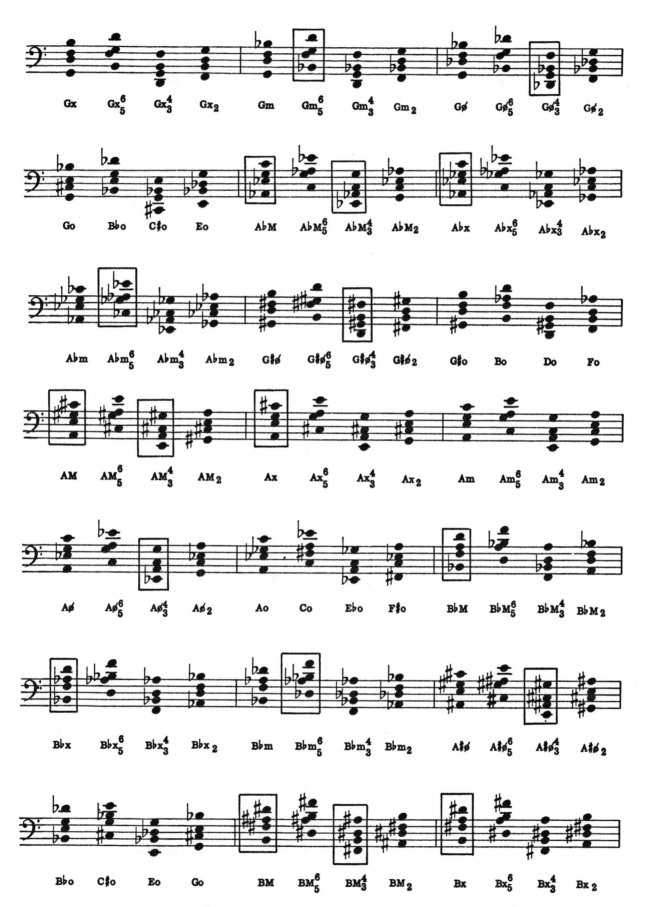

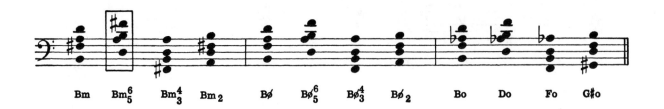

Bm   Bm$_5^6$ Bm$_3^4$ Bm$_2$ Bø   Bø$_5^6$ Bø$_3^4$ Bø$_2$ Bo   Do   Fo   G♯o

Fig. 2 is a bass line for "As Long As There's Music" in G. Note key changes.

Fig. 2.

pick-up

(G) V$^{=3}$ // II$_2$ / I IV // (E) II / V // (D) II V / I IV //

(B) II / V / I // (G) III VIx / II / V$^{=3}$ / II$_2$ / I IV // (E) II /

(E) V // (D) II V / I IV // (B) II / V // (G) III ♭IIIx / II V /

(G) ♭VIIx / VIx ♯Io / II / ♭IIx / I^{+6} / I^{+6} //

DRILL: Practice Fig. 1, avoiding those chords representing span 3 (as marked by frames), if beyond practical reach.

LESSON 20.

Mixed Positions (Voicings)

An outline of the pianistic devices employed by Tatum would, of course, cover a major portion of the history of piano literature, from 1930 to 1950. A specific survey of jazz resources reveals the use of the following tools:

1. Arpeggio-scale techniques (both right and left hand), as studied in Volume I.

2. Swing bass

3. Scale-tone tenth chords:
   a. Root-tenth.
   b. Root-fifth-tenth.
   c. Root-seventh-tenth.
   d. Full scale-tone tenth chord.

4. The complete inversion system of all elements listed in step three.

5. Mixed positions (voicings) — this refers to integrated two-hand voicings used extensively in both rhythmic and ad lib playing. The principle of mixed positions consists of building any number of voicing possibilities between the bass note of a chord (root or inversion) and the melody note.

In building mixed positions the student should closely follow the functions of the tones comprising any chord.

1. Essential tones:

   a. bass note
   b. melody note
   c. third
   d. fifth on φ, o chords
   e. seventh

Aside from the bass and melody notes, the *essential tones* are those revealing the basic qualities (M, x, m, φ, o) of any chord — the *sine qua non* of any tonal arrangement, within the limits of diatonic harmony. The perfect fifth is not a color (*quality indicating*) tone; the diminished fifth appearing in φ and o chords is a color tone.

2. Ornamental tones:

Chord	Tones
Major	9 - ♯11
Dominant	9 - ♭9 - ♯9
	11 (♯3) - ♯11
	13 - ♭13
Minor	9 - 11
Half-diminished	9 - 11
Diminished	9 - 11

It is apparent that the dominant chord offers the most possibilities for ornamentation due to the overtones formed by the interval combination M3, P5, m7.

The following rules are basic to all jazz voicing:

(a) All three ninths (9, ♭9, ♯9) are "self-supporting" (this means the ninth does not need the presence of either the eleventh or the thirteenth to create a complete voicing). In jazz parlance as it applies to *ornamental tones* (9, 11, 13), flatted is synonymous with lowered (♭) and augmented with raised (♯). *Any characterization of ornamental tones* in no way refers to the *quality* of the chord.

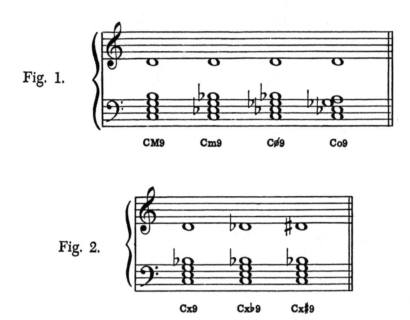

(b) The augmented eleventh (♯11) on the major chords and the eleventh on the minor half-diminished and diminished chords *must* be "supported" by the ninth. (Fig. 3).

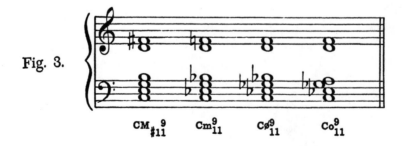

If, in a dominant chord, a tone appears a perfect fourth above the root (in any octave), it is considered a #3 (suspended dominant) if not accompanied by a ninth.

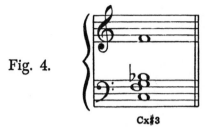

Fig. 4.

Cx#3

Accompanied by either the ninth or the flatted ninth, this tone becomes an eleventh (Fig. 5). (The augmented ninth is not permissible here, since it forms a minor 9-11 chord.)

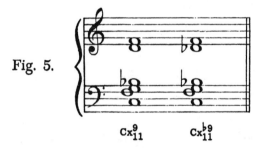

Fig. 5.

Cx_{11}^{9} Cx_{11}^{b9}

In a dominant chord containing a tone a diminished fifth above the root (in any octave), the tone is considered a b5 (altered dominant) if not accompanied by a ninth.

Fig. 6.

Cxb5

Accompanied by a ninth, a flatted ninth, or an augmented ninth, this tone becomes an augmented eleventh (Fig. 7). (The augmented eleventh is avoided in the bass clef for voicing clarity.)

Fig. 7.

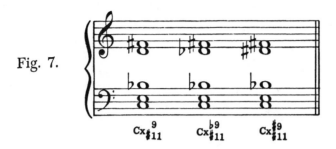

The thirteenth appears only in the dominant chord. In Fig. 8 the function of the 6th tone of the scale in each chord quality is illustrated:

Major: added sixth
Dominant: thirteenth
Minor: added sixth
Half-diminished: non-functional
Diminished: diminished seventh

Fig. 8.

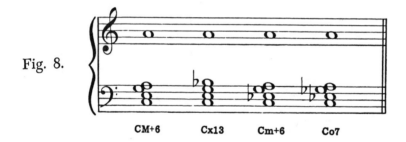

The thirteenth is usually supported by either the ninth, flatted ninth, or augmented ninth (Fig. 9).

Fig. 9.

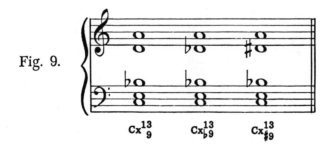

The flatted thirteenth (♭13) *must* be supported by one of the three ninths (Fig. 10).

Fig. 10.

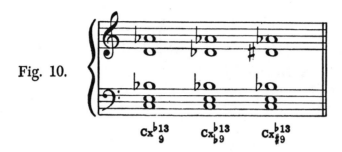

The eleventh or augmented eleventh (♯11) *may* be added to certain harmonic structures containing ninths or thirteenths (Fig. 11).

Fig. 11.

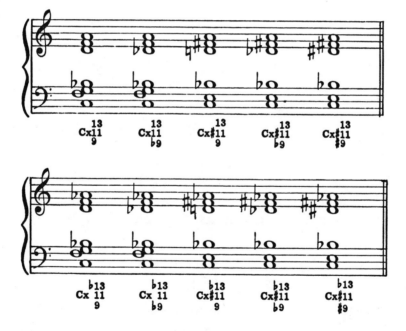

In Figures 1-11 we have considered only several of many voicings for the five chord qualities in which the bass note is C, the melody, one of several tones. The possibilities are probably infinite; however, the student can gradually build up his own resources by ad lib explorations of the numerous melodies and bass lines in Volumes I, II and III, following the application of the *essential* and *ornamental* tones described in this lesson — *each chord must contain*:

root, third, seventh, melody   *fifth* on all half-diminished and diminished chords.

Fig. 12 is a bass line for "Time After Time" in the key of D.

Fig. 12.

I VI / II V$^{\sharp 3}$ / III VI / II V$^{\sharp 3}$ / I / IV / VII / $\flat$VIIx /

VI VI$_2$ / $\flat$Vϕ IVx / III$^{\sharp\sharp 7}$ III$^{\sharp 7}$ / IIIϕ $\flat$IIIx / II$^{\sharp\sharp 7}$ / II$^{\sharp 7}$ /

II / V$^{\sharp 3}$ / I VI / II V$^{\sharp 3}$ / III VI / II V$^{\sharp 3}$ / I VI / Vm $\flat$V / IV /

IVm $\flat$VIIx / VI / IIϕ $_4^{}$ / VI$_2$ / $\flat$Vϕ IVm / III $\flat$IIIo / II $\flat$IIx / I^{+6} /

I^{+6} //

TIME AFTER TIME — by Sammy Cahn and Jule Styne
Sands Music Corp.
Used by permission.

DRILL: Using Figs. 1 to 11 explore various mixed positions on the twelve tones.

LESSON 21.

Mixed Position — Scale-Arpeggio Factors — Left Hand

One of Tatum's most startling devices was the use of scale-arpeggio figures in the left hand to support a right-hand voicing. This meant that the harmonic responsibility, except for the root, passed entirely to the right hand.

LEFT HAND	RIGHT HAND
Root	Third
Scale-Arpeggio	Fifth (optional)
	Seventh
	Melody
	Ornamental Tones

In initially dealing with these devices it is well to begin the left-hand figure on the root and then proceed through the scale-arpeggio figure employing the elements studied in Volume I.

In each melodic position the right-hand voicing is built *down* from the melody, until the essential tones are represented; the root and any accompanying devices appear in the left hand.

Fig. 1 is a harmonization of "Black Magic" in the Key of B♭ based on this technique. The student must add the melody of "Black Magic" as a top voice in the right hand. If the melody note falls on the third or seventh of the prevailing chord, the tone performs both functions simultaneously, *e.g.*, in bar 1, the D melody tone is also the third of the I chord.

Fig. 1.

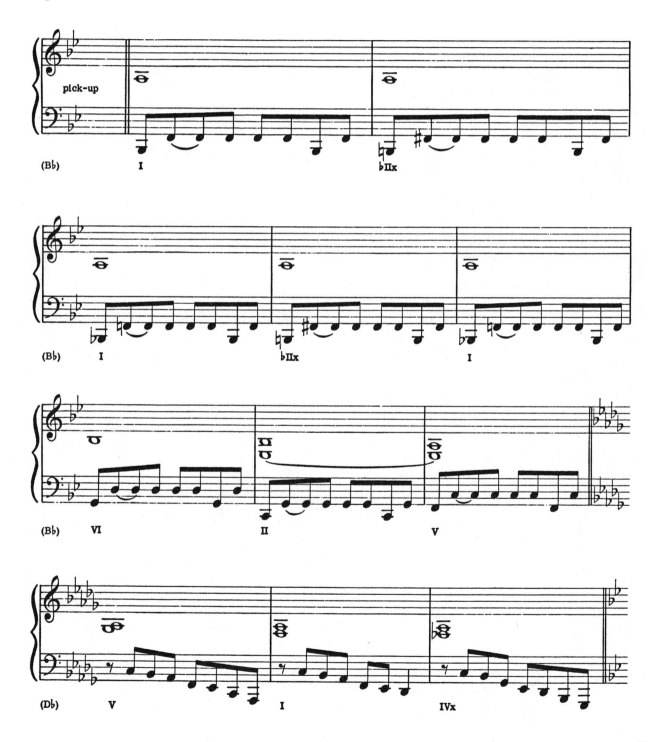

(B♭)   Vm♯7   Vm   ♭V

(B♭)   IV   IVm

Pedal Point

(B♭)   IVm   II   III   IVm   ♭VIIx   III
                                                           V

    ♭IIIo   II
(B♭)   V   V

    IIø   IIø   IIx
(B♭)   V   V   V

DRILL: Explore other melodies applying this technique.

LESSON 22.

Mixed Positions — Axis of the Third and Seventh

Still another important architectural device employed in mixed positions is that of the axis of the third and seventh in Lessons 68, 69, and 70 of Volume I. The principle of the axis is simply one of placing the root and fifth in the left hand; the third, seventh, melody, and selected ornamental tones in the right hand. Fig. 1 illustrates the scale-tone seventh chords of C — axis of the seventh (seventh is the top voice).

Fig. 1.

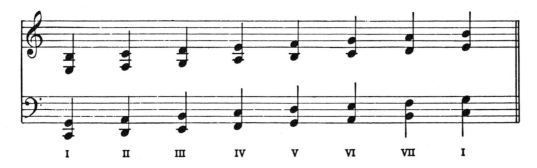

Fig. 2 illustrates the scale-tone seventh chords of G — axis of the third (third is the top voice).

Fig. 2.

The principle involved here is a simple one: build *down* from the melody to the nearest third and seventh or seventh and third *immediately below the melody tone;* add the root and fifth in the left hand.

Occasionally, the student will find that melodic tones accompanying a harmonic unit (half-note or whole-note chord) move through *both* axes; since the melodic phrase must be pursued to its conclusion, the student must *change to the opposite axis* at one of the "on beat" points of the bar (Fig. 3).

Fig. 3.

Fig. 4 is a harmonization in open position, employing both axes, of "Darn That Dream" in the key of A.

Fig. 4.

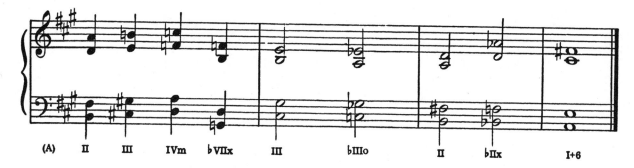

(A)	II	III	IVm	♭VIIx	III	♭IIIo	II	♭IIx	I+6

DARN THAT DREAM — Lyric by Eddie Delange — Music by Jimmy Van Heusen
Copyright 1939 by Bregman, Vocco and Conn, Inc., 1619 Broadway, New York, N. Y.
Used by permission.

DRILL: Practice the scale-tone seventh chords in both axes, through the twelve keys.

LESSON 23.

Mixed Positions
3-7-3 (Major 3rd — minor 7th)
x-x-x circle pattern

One of the fundamental devices of ad lib jazz piano is the left-hand inner voice movement discussed in Lesson 72, Volume I. Fig. 1 below illustrates the basic inner movement of all jazz or diatonic (they are synonymous) harmony — the *third* becoming the *seventh* and the *seventh* becoming the *third* when joined with a circle of fifths.

Fig. 1.

The movement illustrated in Fig. 1 is called a perfect circle of fifths pattern, since the lower voice moves down a perfect fifth or up a perfect fourth. Fig. 2 illustrates the same intervals in an alternate circle of fifths pattern (lower voice moves down a perfect fifth and up an augmented fourth).

Fig. 2.

These intervals represent fragments of chords, the missing elements (*essential, melodic, ornamental*) to be added to the right hand. The fingering in all cases is usually 1-5 for sevenths and 1-2 for thirds.

In the case of Figs. 1 and 2, the implied chords are as follows:

INTERVAL	IMPLIED CHORD
Major 3rd	Major
	Dominant
Minor 7th	Dominant
	Minor
	Half-diminished

Possible circle patterns:

M-x-M

M-m-M

M-φ-M

x-x-x

x-m-x

x-φ-x

The most common of these circle patterns is *x-x-x*. By displacing the third to a tenth, Tatum developed the following left-hand sequences

Fig. 3.

Cx Fx Bbx Ebx Abx Dbx Gbx Bx Ex Ax Dx Gx Cx

Since Fig. 3 employs every unit of span 3, it will be of little practical value to the average student, although it remains one of the most thrilling sounds ever played by a jazz pianist.

Fig. 4 illustrates the circle pattern of Fig. 1 originating on the major thirds of the remaining eleven keys. The student should also explore Fig. 2 originating on the major thirds of the remaining eleven keys.

Fig. 4.

DRILL: All of the circle patterns listed in the above should be explored with the missing voices (*essential, melodic, ornamental*) added to the right hand (see Fig. 5).

Fig. 5.

| Cx9 | Fx13 | B♭x9 | E♭x13 | A♭x9 | D♭x13 | G♭x9 | Bx13 | Ex9 | Ax13 | Dx9 | Gx13 | Cx9 |

Fig. 6 is a harmonization for "Prelude To A Kiss" in E♭ employing the *x-x-x* circle pattern. The melody should be added by the student as a top voice in the right hand.

In *x-x-x* circle patterns, both the minor seventh and major third imply the dominant chord; it is well to begin the series with the interval that will center the left hand in the area of an octave below middle C.

Fig. 6.

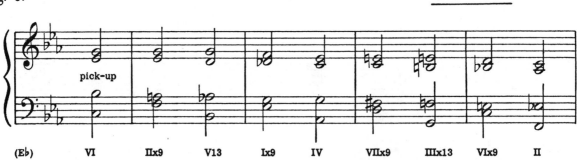

| (E♭) | VI | IIx9 | V13 | Ix9 | IV | VIIx9 | IIIx13 | VIx9 | II |

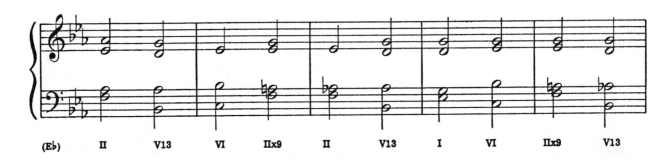

| (E♭) | II | V13 | VI | IIx9 | II | V13 | I | VI | IIx9 | V13 |

PRELUDE TO A KISS — Copyright 1938 by American Academy of Music, Inc.
Used by permission.

Mixed Positions
7-3-7 (minor 7th — major 3rd)
m-x-m circle patterns

Fig. 1 illustrates the reverse of Fig. 1, Lesson 23, Although the principle of seven becoming three and three becoming seven is still maintained. Fig. 1 represents the perfect circle of fifths patterns; Fig. 2, the alternate circle of fifths pattern.

Fig. 1.

Fig. 2.

In Figs. 1 and 2, the implied chords are as follows:

INTERVAL	IMPLIED CHORD
Minor 7th	Dominant
	Minor
	Half-diminished
Major 3rd	Major
	Dominant

possible circle patterns:

x-M-x
m-M-m
φ-M-φ
x-x-x
m-x-m
φ-x-φ

Of these, the most common circle patterns are the last two. Fig. 3 illustrates the *m-x-m* circle pattern expanded into open position. Fig. 3 employs only spans 1 and 2, which places it within the reach of every pianist.

Fig. 3.

Fig. 4 illustrates the circle pattern in Fig. 1 originating on the minor sevenths of the remaining eleven keys. The student should also explore Fig. 2 originating on the minor sevenths of the remaining eleven keys.

Fig. 4.

Explore circle patterns listed above in closed and open position, if possible adding the missing voices (essential, melodic, ornamental) in the right hand (see Fig. 5).

Fig. 5

Fig. 6 is a harmonization for "Satin Doll" in E employing the *m-x-m* circle pattern. The melody should be added as a top voice in the right hand. "Satin Doll," employs the *m-x-m* circle pattern in interrupted fragments: *m-x, m-x,* etc. These fragments should be thought of as an incomplete II-V pattern, creating a harmonic tension which is finally resolved in the seventh bar.

Fig. 6

II V / II V / III VIx / III VIx / VI IIx / ♭VI ♭IIx / I II /

III VI / II V / II V / III VIx / III VIx / VI IIx / ♭VI ♭IIx /

I II / III ♯IVo / Vm Ix / Vm ♭V / IV Vm / VI ♭VIIm / VI IIx /

VI ♭VIx / V IV / III ♭IIIo / II V / II V / III VIx / III VIx /

VI IIx / ♭VI ♭IIx / I / I //

SATIN DOLL — Duke Ellington, Billy Strayhorn & Johnny Mercer
Copyright 1958 by Tempo Music, Inc.
Used by permission in U.S.A. & Canada only.

In using this device, the missing factors (essential tones, melody, ornamental tones) must be added to the right hand. There are two possible combinations in Fig. 6.

LEFT HAND	RIGHT HAND
root-seventh	melody—third
root-third	melody—seventh—flatted ninth

In *m-x-m* circle patterns, the minor chord is always indicated by the minor seventh, the dominant chord by the major third. The same is true of *ϕ-x-ϕ* circle pattern.

DRILL: Practice Fig. 1 through 5 for automatic facility.

LESSON **25.**

Mixed Positions
7-3-7 (Minor 7th — major 3rd)
φ-x-φ circle pattern

The φ-x-φ circle pattern is built on the identical intervals appearing in Fig. 1, Lesson 24, except that the diminished fifth (for φ) must appear in the right hand (see Fig. 1).

Fig. 1.

Gφ   Cx$_9^{13}$ Fφ   Bbx$_9^{13}$ D#φ   Abx$_9^{13}$ C#φ   F#x$_9^{13}$ Bφ   Ex$_9^{13}$ Aφ   Dx$_9^{13}$

The φ-x-φ circle pattern should be explored from the various points of origin illustrated in Lesson 24, Fig. 4, adding the necessary tones (essential, melodic, ornamental) to the right hand.

Fig. 2 is a harmonization for "Woodyn' You" in Ab. The *front* phrase of this tune is built on a φ-x-φ fragment; the bridge employs a *m-x-m* fragment similar to the *front* strain of "Satin Doll."

Fig. 2.

bVφ / VIIx / IIIφ / VIx / IIφ / V / I II / VI$^{4}_{3}$ IV / bVφ /

VIIx / IIIφ / VIx / IIφ / V / I II / VI$^{4}_{3}$ #IVo / Vm Ix / Vm Ix /

Vm bV / IV / VI IIx / VI IIx / VI bVIx / V / bVφ / VIIx /

IIIφ / VIx / IIφ / V / I^{+6} / I^{+6} //

WOODYN' YOU —
© Copyright 1943, Charling Music Corporation
Used by permission.

DRILL: Explore φ-x-φ patterns from all twelve tones of the chromatic scale.

88

Swing Bass

Tatum's swing bass has none of the architectural symmetry of Wilson; nor do the hands move in the interrelated geometric design that characterizes the Wilson style.

In Tatum's system, swing bass is only one of a multitude of elements brought to bear on an improvisation. Often the full tenth is not "swung," but simply acts as a harmonic underpinning for a linear rhythmic pattern appearing in the right hand. The following ten studies (Chapters 26 through 35) will present modified swing-bass examples in the general idiom of Tatum. Span 3 is excluded. Swing chords will be identified with those studied in Lessons 7 through 11. A substitute voicing will be introduced in these studies to *cover* the dominant chords occurring in span 3. This voicing consists of a root, major 3rd, minor 7th, and one of the ninths (ninth, flatted ninth, augmented ninth) (Fig. 1 to 4). From these studies it is hoped that the student may capture, in spite of the constantly shifting architecture of his style, what remains probably the essential "sound" of the Tatum concept.

Fig. 1.

Fig. 2.

Fig. 3.

Fig. 4

Fig. 5 is a modified harmonization to "April in Paris" in C. Improvise in the right hand on Fig. 5.

Fig. 5.

APRIL IN PARIS —
Copyright 1932 by Harms, Inc.
Used by permission.

NOTE: In this and the following nine studies, the student may create his own swing-bass structures from the half-note harmony. However, it should be remembered that improvisation is assumed to be present in the right hand and the student should avoid overplaying. These studies, however, do allow for optional variations so long as the bass line remains intact.

DRILL: It is suggested at this point that the student begin a systematic study of the piano literature of the nineteenth and twentieth centuries in order to better understand the classical resources of Tatum's conception. This knowledge, joined with the material presented in this volume will enable the student to deal with the basic stylistic idioms of this great master.

Pedaling

Tatum's exquisite control of the piano extended to the brilliant use of the sustaining (loud) pedal. In studies such as those appearing in Lessons 26 to 35, pedaling is determined by the relationship of tonal elements existing in both hands. Tatum could actually project a feeling of having pedaled the left hand and not the right.

The rule here is to allow the right hand to determine the question of pedaling. Studies such as these under consideration allow for extended "space" in the right hand, which means that large sections of the left-hand architecture permit the pedaling of each harmonic unit to insure a smooth, legato "walking" sound. Swing-bass elements (tenth-chord) are treated as a single unit.

Any extended horizontal figures in the right hand automatically exclude pedaling.

A unique aspect of Tatum's pedaling technique was the impressionistic device of "catching" the vibrating strings immediately after the keys have been released. This device is more effective in slow ad lib playing in which full advantage can be taken of their pedaled sonorities.

Fig. 1 is a modified harmonization of "Imagination" in G. Improvise on Fig. 1.

Fig. 1.

DRILL: Practice Fig. 1 as well as previous studies, pedaling each harmonic unit (tenth-swing chord) for smoothness of pulse.

LESSON 28.

"Intros"

The usual introduction employed in a jazz performance is a two or four-bar sequence of chords moving in half or whole-notes. The purpose of an "intro" is two-fold.

1. to establish a key center
2. to establish a pulse

An orderly pattern of chords is usually chosen to lead smoothly into the initial chord of the tune. Some improvisational material is introduced into the right hand in order to sustain rhythmic and melodic interest above the prevailing chords.

Obviously the initial chord of the tune determines to a large extent the character of the "intro." Since the bulk of jazz tunes begins on the I, II, or VI chord, it is possible to indicate a number of patterns suitable for these three categories.

Tunes starting on the I chord:

$$III \; \flat IIIx \; / \; II \; \flat IIx \; //$$
$$III \; / \; \flat IIIx \; / \; II \; / \; \flat IIx \; //$$
$$I \; VI \; / \; II \; V \; //$$
$$I \; / \; VI \; / \; II \; / \; V \; //$$
$$\flat V\phi \; IVm \; / \; III \; \flat IIIx \; / \; II \; / \; \flat IIx \; //$$
$$I^{+6} \; Ix_2 \; / \; II_4 \; \flat VIx \; / \; VI_2 \; / \; \flat IIx \; //$$
$$VI_2 \; / \; VI_2 \; / \; VI_2 \; / \; II \; \flat IIx \; //$$

Tunes starting on the II chord:

$$I \; / \; \sharp Io \; //$$
$$\flat V\phi \; IVm \; / \; III \; \flat IIIx \; //$$
$$\flat V\phi \; / \; IVm \; / \; III \; / \; \flat IIIx \; //$$
$$I^{+6} \; Ix_2 \; / \; II_4 \; \flat VIx \; / \; VI_2 \; IV \; / \; III \; \flat IIIx \; //$$
$$V \; IV \; / \; III \; \flat IIIx \; //$$
$$V \; / \; IV \; / \; III \; / \; \flat IIIx \; //$$

Tunes starting on the VI chord:

$$I \; IV \; / \; VII \; IIIx \; //$$
$$I \; / \; IV \; / \; VII \; / \; IIIx \; //$$
$$VI \; \flat V\phi \; / \; VII \; \flat VIIx \; // \; \text{see Note (1)}$$
$$VI \; / \; \flat V\phi \; / \; VII \; / \; IIIx \; // \; \text{see Note (2)}$$
$$IIIx \; IIIx_2 \; / \; \flat V\phi_4 \; IIIx_4 \; //$$
$$IIIx \; / \; VIIm_4 \; / \; Vo \; / \; IIIx_6 \; //$$

In tunes employing an initial chord other than I, II or VI, a basic intro of I VI II V of the prevailing key is suggested — then proceed immediately to the initial chord.

Note (1) Im VI / II ♭IIx // in minor scale-tone chords

Note (2) Im / VI / II / V // in minor scale-tone chords

All of these formations should be played in some expanded form (displaced third, etc.).

Fig. 1 is a modified harmonization for "Stella by Starlight" in C major. Improvise on Fig. 1.

Fig. 1.

STELLA BY STARLIGHT — by Ned Washington and Victor Young
© 1946 Famous Music Corp., New York, N. Y.
Used by permission.

DRILL: Practice the "intros" appearing in this lesson in the various keys
employing tenths, swing bass and mixed positions.

Melody

Tatum's persistent concern for the melodic fabric of a tune has long been a controversial element of his general style. It is important to understand that the simple problem facing the horn man in "blowing" a single note line on a set of harmonic changes, was a highly intensified problem to Tatum in the Thirties, who was attempting to transform the entire classical literature of the piano into the new context of an emerging art form.

Traditional classical music has largely been based on thematic development (melodic improvisation) usually sustained by an underpinning of chordal-arpeggio-scale elements (harmonic improvisation).

This great idiomatic tradition had to be explored thoroughly in order that future jazz pianists might build on a permanent evaluation of the role of this tradition in jazz.

Furthermore, previous explorations in the area of extracting classical resources for use in jazz by Morton, Hines, and Waller had not exceeded the harmonic devices of early Romanticism (Beethoven and Schubert). In the early Thirties there existed a desperate need for continuing these explorations through later 19th century Romanticism into 20th century Impressionism.

This was Tatum's achievement. If he sometimes seemed to deal with inflexible, uncongenial classical idioms it was to ascertain thoroughly their eventual value to the jazz pianist.

When working with these later classical idioms, (Chopin, Schumann, Brahms and Debussy), it was quite natural for Tatum to employ the melody as a cohesive device. It must also be kept in mind that Tatum was essentially a solo pianist, which meant that the melody along with the pulse and harmony of a tune represented an important source of inspiration in this extremely difficult idiom.

Fig. 1 is a modified harmonization of "Can't We Be Friends." Improvise on Fig. 1.

Fig. 1.

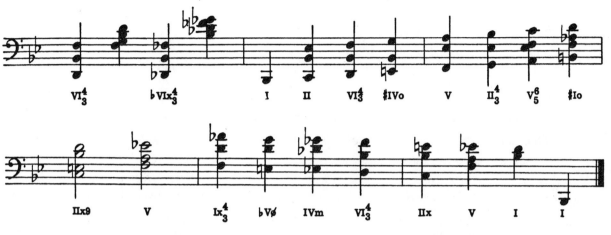

CAN'T WE BE FRIENDS —
Copyright 1929 by Harms, Inc.
Used by permission.

DRILL: The student is advised to begin a thorough research through documentary and anthology recordings of James P. Johnson, Willie "The Lion" Smith and Thomas "Fats" Waller in order to become familiar with the important predecessors of Tatum.

LESSON 30.

The Harlem School

Previous to Tatum, the history of jazz piano is essentially a panorama of various "regional" explorations of classical forms and their application to the jazz format. These various regional schools were as follows:

The South:	New Orleans
	Mobile
	Shreveport
	Memphis
	Baton Rouge
The Mid-West:	Chicago
	Kansas City
	Sedalia
	Toledo
The East:	New York (Harlem)
	Pittsburgh
	Baltimore
	Philadelphia

The various influences of jazz piano were: barrel house
rags
blues
boogie woogie
minstrels
medicine shows
vaudeville

Of the above-mentioned centers of regional activity, the most pertinent to Tatum was the **Harlem School of the Twenties.** The important styles explored by this school were ragtime and minstrels. One of the favorite pastimes of these pianists was what they called "raggin' the classics," revamping romantic bravura pieces with "stride" bass figures. "Striding" was a left-hand swing-bass device — playing a single note in the deep bass followed by a quick transference to a chord in the center of the keyboard. These pianists also explored decorative arrangements of popular tunes laden with *bravura* octaves, sixths, and thirds, as found in classical drill books. These can be heard on many piano rolls. Here can be found episodic passages characteristic of the Chopin mazurkas, the Schubert impromptus, the Beethoven sonatas.

From the Harlem school emerged an important line of descent stemming from Lucky Roberts through James P. Johnson to Fats Waller, whom Tatum considered his main source of influence.

Early recordings by Tatum display the same florid exhibitionism as was found in the Harlem school; yet without these explorations the way would not have been paved for Tatum's eventual distillation, to form the brilliant architecture of "swing" piano.

Fig. 1 is a modified harmonization of "Smoke Gets In Your Eyes" in the key of D

Fig. 1.

100

LESSON 31.

Fats Waller

Tatum always maintained that his basic influence was Fats Waller. Since Waller represented the final link in the Harlem school, this is essentially correct. It could also mean that Tatum felt that the essence of his style lay in his left hand (Waller) rather than his right hand (Hines).

Certainly Waller's right hand could hardly have been of importance to Tatum, with its tiresome ragtime idioms and tricks completely devoid of any linear "horn" concept.

James P. Johnson was the first recorded pianist to use the tenth instead of the single note (*stride*), the octave (*early ragtime*), or the sixth (*fifth and third of the chord*) employed by Morton.

Waller expanded Johnson's tenth patterns into a highly complex system; he also introduced the pedal as an important adjunct connecting the units.

The resonance achieved by Waller in his left hand could at times be thunderous when joined by his vertically (*chorded*) oriented right hand.

Waller had been a church organist and from the Bach chorales had acquired a deep insight into precise voice leading and the value of a legato "swing," rather than the hitherto staccato attack of ragtime.

Waller was also an entertainer but, unlike Morton, made everything subservient to his playing. Waller's "hard" swing innovated ideas concerning the jazz beat, especially in an abandonment of the older idiom of the "dead space" between pulses. Waller's "connected" pulses were important in leading to the *legato* concept of modern jazz piano. His influence on Tatum remains primary.

Fig. 1 is a modified harmonization of "Everything Happens To Me" in the key of E♭.

Fig. 1.

102

EVERYTHING HAPPENS TO ME — Words: Tom Adair — Music: Matt Dennis
Copyright 1941 Embassy Music Corporation. All rights reserved.
Used by permission of the copyright owner.

DRILL: Employ a legato, pedaled touch in Fig. 1.

LESSON 32.

Earle Hines

Earle Hines freed the right hand from the mechanical restriction of
ragtime, paving the way for the linear concepts of Tatum. Hines adapted
a fast octave technique in order to achieve a keyboard version of the *horn*
lines as played by trumpeter Louis Armstrong, clarinetist Jimmy Noone,
and tenor saxophonist "Stomp" Evans.

Except for some small group recordings made by Hines with Armstrong's "Hot Five" and "Hot Seven," Hines worked within the format of
the large band. Working within this format created certain advantages.
These included a strong rhythm section, releasing Hines from any left-
hand responsibility and allowing for a complete concentration on the right-

hand octave "horn" line. This aided Hines in forging a new image as to the role of the piano within a rhythm section, a disciplined role subordinated to the work of the over-all section, rather than the previous "waterfall" (arhythmic arpeggio) style.

As a solo pianist, Tatum was not primarily interested in this aspect of Hines's playing, but the right-hand "trumpet" style of Hines certainly remained an important source for Tatum's linear ideas.

One of the few solo recordings made by Hines, his "57 Varieties" recorded in 1928, is a startling revelation of what was to occur in jazz piano for the succeeding ten years. Here can be heard a musical preview of the later development of Joe Sullivan, Jess Stacy, Teddy Wilson, and, of course, Tatum.

Earle Hines remains one of the great giants in the crowded history of jazz piano.

Fig. 1 is a modified harmonization of three choruses of the traditional 12-bar blues. Improvise on Fig. 1.

Fig. 1.

DRILL: Employ a legato, pedaled touch in Fig. 1.

LESSON 33.

Right-Hand Components

Unlike Wilson, who forged an entire architecture from two basic rhythmic units (quarters in the left hand, eighth-notes in the right), Tatum utilized the rhythmic gamut, from the whole-note to the sixty-fourth note.

Both Hines and Morton explored aspects of this gamut, but until Tatum, the bravura levels of time were more the province of horn men than pianists. (This discussion excludes arhythmic arpeggiation of the "waterfall" school.)

Previous right-hand levels had generally been restricted to the half, quarter, and eighth-notes. Pre-Tatum punctuation (rest-values) was usually limited to larger units — whole-rest, half-rest, quarter-rest; bravura punctuation elements values — sixteenth, thirty-second, sixty-fourth rests — were usually avoided, since pre-Tatum technical levels did not permit the rhythmic precision for these values.

Tatum's explorations in this area, together with similar developments by Roy Eldridge and Coleman Hawkins, established the basis for the rhythmic revolution of the Forties, dominated by Bud Powell and Charlie Parker.

Tatum's right-hand conceptions employed various rhythmic units in surprising juxtapositions, sometimes as "fills" between melodic fragments, sometimes as melodic phrases played in diminution (quickened values), sometimes as scale-arpeggio material based on the chordal elements.

In general, the levels established by Tatum still are maintained in present day virtuoso jazz piano (Peterson, Peiffer, Newborn). A breakdown of the units employed in the three main tempos is as follows:

1. Ballad
2. Bounce
3. Fast.

Fig. 1 is a modified harmonization of "How About You" in A♭. Improvise on Fig. 1.

Fig. 1.

106

DRILL: Employ a legato, pedaled touch in Fig. 1.

LESSON 34.

Walking — Bass Lines

Tatum's walking bass lines remain to this day a marvel of harmonic ingenuity, impeccable voice-leading, and architectural perfection. Quarter-note harmony was virtually unknown before Tatum's day, and strangely enough has disappeared in present-day playing with the exception of the "walking" lines played by contemporary bass players.

The half-note unit of harmony was, of course, essential to the modern rhythmic composite after 1940, yet one cannot help but regret the disappearance of Tatum's rich panorama of harmonic color.

Tatum's walking bass lines fall into the following traditional categories:

1. Circles of fifths

Circles of fifths patterns are, of course, usually explicit in a bass line; it remained for Tatum to mount them architecturally. In Fig 1, one extension of this axiom, however, is illustrated in bars 11 and 12 in which a circle pattern has been "backed up" to create a longer line. This device is generally subservient to what are known as the "pivot" chords of a tune — chords appearing on the first beat of the odd bars (1, 3, 5, 7, etc). These pivot chords must be respected, if the fabric of the tune is to be preserved, but they may be "approached" through the even bars (2, 4, 6, 8, etc.) with material not originally pertinent to those bars.

2. Diatonic progressions

Diatonic (major scale) progressions usually proceed through the prevailing mode step-wise ascending or descending. These progressions also are subservient to the pivot chords.

3. Chromatic "approaches"

Pivot chords are often approached a half-step above or below, to lend tension to the bass line. The most common qualities used in these approach chords are the dominant and the diminished (see Fig. 1 — bars 1, 3, 4, 5, 9, 13, 14, and 15).

These walking lines account to a large extent for Tatum's "setting" his improvisations into arrangements which were played almost identically in each performance. There are many things to be said for this. These arrangements never sounded as if they were set, which is a feat in itself. They represented a distillation of the *very best* after years of exploration; the delicacy of the balance between the hands made an arrangement almost imperative. Tatum finally emerged as a pianist no longer dealing with the arbitrary relationships of an improvisation, but rather with a congealed perfection, which may be called absolute.

Fig. 1 is a modified harmonization for "I've Got A Crush On You" in E. Improvise on Fig. 1.

Fig. 1.

108

DRILL: Employ a legato, pedaled touch in Fig. 1.

LESSON 35.

Classical Form — Jazz Content

The technique of placing jazz conceptions in a classical framework has been, from the beginning, a serious problem for the jazz musician. The history of jazz offers ample proof of the truism, that the greatest jazz has organically created its own design rather than taking on a ready-made form.

One of the most startling aspects of Tatum's genius was his ability to use a classical form as an exciting frame for jazz ideas. The main sources of Tatum's formal "conversion" were Chopin, Liszt, Brahms, and the Impressionists (Debussy and Ravel).

In rhythmic passages it is a fairly simple problem to generate a jazz feeling, but to sustain this feeling in arhythmic passages, through only the devices of phrasing and voicing is extremely difficult, yet one with which Tatum dealt with consummate skill.

Tatum's use of the tenth helped to create much of the idiomatic jazz timbre of his style. He employed impressionistic idioms but within the framework of strict diatonic voice-leading.

Tatum's early period (1930-1938) reveals a struggle to apply difficult classical piano idioms to jazz. By the middle period (1938-1945), from which much of the material of this section is taken, it is evident that the master pianist had forged a new, clear image; the classical edges are gone. The latter period (1945 until his death in 1957) is a brilliant documentation of Tatum's gradual extension of his pianistic architecture into the periphery of polytonality and atonality, anticipating the entire spectrum of the harmonic explorations of contemporary jazz. Bud Powell's "Poco Loco" and "Glass Enclosure" can be traced directly to this final period of Tatum.

Fig. 1 is a modified harmonization of "I Gotta Right To Sing The Blues" in D♭. Improvise on Fig. 1.

Fig. 1.

DRILL: Employ a legato, pedaled touch in Fig. 1, remembering that the appearance of a new chord necessitates a pedaling stroke.

LESSON 36.

Harmonic Fragmentation — Circles of Fifths

Powell's contribution to modern jazz piano was discussed in Lesson 72 of Volume I. In solving the basic problem of abandoning swing bass and transferring the rigid vertical structure of previous swing piano into a more flowing linear form, Powell laid the foundation for much of jazz piano's stylistic techniques since the early Forties and has remained the primary influence of all succeeding pianists. The major achievements of George Shearing, Horace Silver, and Oscar Peterson can be traced to Powell's architecture. It is important that the student be aware of a functional innovation begun by Tatum and completed by Powell, namely: *placing the rhythmic pulse in the right hand while reducing the left hand to a harmonic underpinning.*

There are three basic left hand designs to be considered here: 1. Circles of fifths patterns. 2. Diatonic patterns. 3. Chromatic patterns.

1. Circles of fifths patterns:
   x-x-x- circle — see Lesson 23, Figs. 1, 2, 5
   m-x-m circle — see Lesson 24, Figs. 1, 2, 5
   ϕ-x-ϕ circle — same as m-x-m

Complete facility with these circle of fifth patterns is essential to mastering the Powell style. Unlike Lessons 23 and 24, these harmonic "fragments" will constitute the only vertical structure in either hand; the "implied" tones of any fragment will appear only in the right hand improvised line.

This device is described as "harmonic fragmentation," since in any chord only the root-third or root-seventh appear in the left hand; the remaining voices (*seventh, fifth, third, melody, ornamental tones*) in the right. Use of the sustaining pedal is prohibited.

If the root-third occurs in the left hand, it is referred to as the *point of three;* if the root-seventh occurs, it is referred to as the *point of seven —* the point is the top voice of the left-hand fragment.

Since the minor seventh interval infers any one of three chords (dominant, minor, half-diminished), the right-hand line must complete the indicated quality (see Fig. 1).

Fig. 1.

All inversions are considered *point of six* (bass and soprano tones of the inversion).

Fig. 2 is a harmonic fragmentation for "Somebody Loves Me" in C. Improvise on Fig. 2.

Fig. 2.

DRILL: Study circle patterns in Chapters 23 and 24.

Harmonic Fragmentation — Diatonic

Diatonic patterns occur only at the *point of seven*. Fig. 1 illustrates the fragments of the scale-tone chords in C. Points follow the scale-tone quality of the chord unless an alteration is indicated.

Fig. 1.

The following table illustrates the various scale-tone chords with their respective point qualities in both THREE and SEVEN.

Chord	Point of 3	Point of 7
I	M	M
II	m	m
III	m	m
IV	M	M
V	x	x
VI	m	m
VII	φ	φ

The student will notice that each point assumes the quality of the *chord*, not of the *interval* (i.e., in V, the major third and the minor seventh both imply a dominant chord, the minor sevenths on II, III, and VI imply minor chords, the minor seventh of V implies dominant, the minor seventh on VII implies half-diminished).

In the Powell system the roots of all *points of seven* appear in the second octave below middle C (see Fig. 2 illustrating the fragments of the key of G).

Fig. 2.

Fig. 3 is a harmonic fragmentation of "Skylark" in G.

Fig. 3.

SKYLARK — Hoagy Carmichael and Johnny Mercer
Copyright 1941 by George Simon, Inc., 1619 Broadway, New York, N. Y.
Used by permission.

DRILL: Practice the scale-tone seventh fragments at the point of seven
in 12 keys. Improvise on Fig. 3.

LESSON 38

Harmonic Fragmentation — Chromatic

Chromatic patterns always appear at the point of seven. The usual chromatic patterns are:

II-♭IIx-I   III-♭IIIx-II-♭IIx-I   I-♯Io-II-♯IIo-III   ♭Vɸ-IVo-III-♭IIIo-II-♭IIx-I

It is understood that these chromatic patterns are substitutes for circle of fifth patterns. The equivalent circle patterns for the above in order are:

7 3 7	7 3 3 7 3 7	7 7 7 3 7	7 3 7 3 7 3 7
II-V-II	III-VIx-II-V-I	I-VIx-II-V-I	♭Vɸ-VIIx-III-VIx-II-V-I

DRILL: Practice the chromatic patterns in all keys for automatic facility. Fig. 1 is a harmonic fragmentation for "Memories Of You" in F. Improvise on Fig. 1.

Fig. 1.

MEMORIES OF YOU — Words by Andy Razaf, Music by Eubie Blake
Copyright MCMXXX and MCMLIV by Shapiro, Bernstein & Co. Inc.
Copyright Renewed MCMLVII and Assigned to Shapiro, Bernstein & Co. Inc.
Used by permission of Shapiro, Bernstein & Co. Inc., 666 Fifth Avenue, New York 19, N.Y.

LESSON 39.

Alternate Circle Patterns

The alternate circle patterns studied in Chapters 23 and 24 comprise an important left-hand device in Powell's system. This device of superimposing a quarter or half-note alternate circle pattern over the normal harmony of a tune is quite simple in its basic technique. If a tune contains a passage allowing for a descending chromatic design such as IIIx-♭IIIx-IIx-♭IIx-I (Fig. 1), simply *prepare* each dominant with a minor or half-diminished chord a perfect fifth above, cutting the time values in half (Fig. 2).

Fig. 1.

Fig. 2.

This device can occasionally be used in the body of a tune; also it can frequently be used in "turn-about" cadences (bars 7, 8, 23, and 24 of normal tunes containing a repeated "front" phrase, a "bridge" and a "front" phrase once again).

A second familiar pattern allowing for the same "preparation" is ♭VIIx-VIx-♭VIx-V (Fig. 3). This preparation appears in Fig. 4.

Fig. 3.

Fig. 4.

DRILL: Practice the following patterns in 12 keys with quarter-note units in the left hand and an eighth-note improvised line in the right.

$$\overset{7}{\text{VIIm}} - \overset{3}{\text{IIIx}} - ♭\overset{7}{\text{VIIm}} - ♭\overset{3}{\text{IIIx}} - \overset{7}{\text{VI}} - \overset{3}{\text{IIx}} - ♭\overset{7}{\text{VI}} - ♭\overset{3}{\text{IIx}} - \overset{7}{\text{I}}$$
and
$$\overset{7}{\text{IVm}} - ♭\overset{3}{\text{VIIx}} - \overset{7}{\text{III}} - \overset{3}{\text{VIx}} - ♭\overset{7}{\text{III}} - ♭\overset{3}{\text{VIx}} - \overset{7}{\text{II}} - \overset{3}{\text{V}} - \overset{7}{\text{I}}$$

Fig. 5 is a modern harmonization for "I Can't Get Started With You" in D, employing the alternate circle pattern. Improvise on Fig. 5.

Fig. 5.

LESSON **40.**

Right Hand Components — Ballad

The rhythmic elements in Powell's line are startlingly simple. If one could say that Wilson had built a completely evolved system employing quarter notes in the left hand and eighths in the right, it can be said with equal validity that Powell accomplished the same task with half-notes in the left hand and eighths in the right.

Powell's right hand units in a ballad tempo (M.M. = 60 − 100) are the eighth and sixteenth. The line also abounds in the use of chromatic (non-modal) tones used to deflect or delay the quality of a chord. Some of Powell's persistent idioms employed in this manner are the following, based on the prevailing mode of the chord.

Major Chord:	Dominant Chord:	Minor Chord:
raised 2nd	raised 2nd	raised 3rd
lowered 2nd	raised 4th	lowered 2nd
raised 4th	lowered 2nd	raised 7th
	raised 7th	raised 4th

Half-diminished Chord:	Diminished Chord:
raised 3rd	raised 7th
lowered 2nd	lowered 2nd
raised 5th	
raised 7th	

Fig. 2 is a bass line for "Angel Eyes" in G minor. The numerals refer to the minor scale-tone chords treated in Section X, Volume I. Fig. 1 illustrates the minor scale-tone chords in G minor. The bridge modulates to E♭ and D major.

Fig. 1.

(g)   ImL   II∅   IIIM+   IVm   Vx   VI∅   VIIo   ImL

Fig. 2.

(g)   ♯7   7   7   6   5   6   7   7   7   7   7
    I   Im   Io   II2   I   Im2   ♭VIx   I   VI   II   ♭IIx

120

DRILL: Explore the chromatic tones listed in the above table, integrating them into scale-arpeggio lines, (see Lesson 55, Vol. I). Improvise on Fig. 2.

LESSON 41.

Right Hand Components — Up Tempo

Powell's up-tempo elements employ the eighth-note almost exclusively with the use of an occasional eighth-note triplet. Rhythmic punctuation (rest values [see Vol. II, pp. 100-102]) is minimized with the use of extended (sometimes up to eight bars), unpunctuated eighth-note lines. When rest values are used, they are often of some length (whole-rest, dotted half-rest) connecting two long phrases.

Also, one of Powell's outstanding melodic characteristics is evident here — building phrases in which the top note of a phrase may fall on any one of eight possible points (eight eighth-notes to a bar). This top tone is always accented, which creates a rhythmic counterpoint sometimes in agreement with the quarter-note foot beat, sometimes in opposition to the foot beat (see Lesson 58, Volume I: also Volume II, pp. 100-102).

Even at break-neck tempos, a melodic lyricism prevails in Powell's lines at all times. These tempos may extend from M.M. $\downarrow$ = 120 to beyond M.M. $\downarrow$ = 300.

Fig. 1 is a bass line for "Indiana" in A. A good tempo for Fig. 1 is M.M. $\downarrow$ = 200 (foot beat).

Fig. 1.

DRILL: Study pages 100-102, Volume II, in order to become acquainted with the musical and technical idioms of Powell's playing.

LESSON **42.**

Setting A Bass Line

It is apparent from a brief survey of the bass lines in this and the previous six lessons that, unlike Wilson and Tatum before him, Powell is not essentially interested in building a constantly improvised bass line. Rather, the line is "set" in order to release the total energies for the melodic and rhythmic achievement in the right-hand line.

Powell's system is not a two-handed integrated architecture as with Wilson and Tatum. One reason for this is the fact that Powell is exclusively a group (*non-solo*) pianist playing a horn line (*essentially non-pianistic*).

Since Powell's left hand devices are so limited (root position intervals of sevenths and thirds) the normal keyboard problems of sonority, voicing, and architectural direction are not present. As a result, the improvisational demands are much more severe since the remaining factors are automatically set.

To reduce the piano to the role of a *single-note horn* was a necessary step taken by Powell in order to rediscover the essentials concealed within the elaborate architecture of Wilson and Tatum. Successive pianists since Powell (Silver, Shearing, Peterson, Hawes), have been able to rebuild the architecture of modern jazz piano on the basis of Powell's evaluation.

Fig. 1 is a bass line for "Early Autumn" in E♭. Improvise on Fig. 1. Note key changes.

Fig. 1.

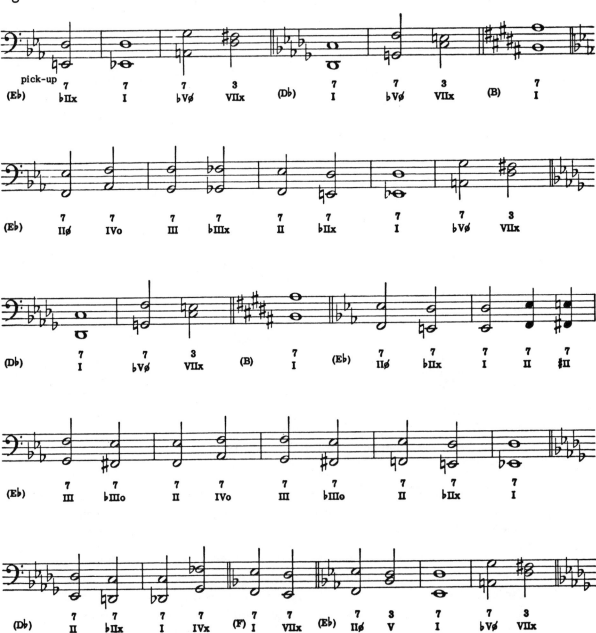

DRILL: When improvising on Fig. 1, use Parker's model of an improvised line on a ballad appearing on pages 109, 110, Volume II. Here the sixteenth note prevails interrupted by the eighth note or its equivalent value — the tied sixteenth.

LESSON 43.

Building a Bass Line

Since everything in a Powell improvisation seems to stem from the "set" bass line or underpinning, it is essential that the student be able to quickly "set" his own bass line.

If we begin with sheet music, the first step is to convert the sheet music elements (lettered symbols, notation) to Roman numerals (see page 201, Volume I). The resulting "solution" is to a jazz musician a special combination of patterns (II-V-I, etc.) appropriate for that particular tune.

The next step is to apply the points of 7-3 architecture to these patterns. Of course, the circle of fifths is preferable to any other pattern (the only pattern in which both 7 and 3 can be used). Next in order would be chromatic patterns and finally diatonic patterns — both employing point of 7 only.

When the bass line and the point of 7-3 architecture are "set," it is well to memorize it (left hand alone) in order to allow the total energies to be directed toward the right hand line.

This "setting" of a bass line is a fairly automatic process with a professional jazz musician — the entire process should take no more than two minutes for a skilled professional. The student will find that as more and more tunes are "set" this way, the process of "jungling" these patterns becomes a fairly simple problem, since each tune employs the same patterns in varying juxtaposition; e.g., in Fig. 3, a jazz musician would break down the bass line into the following segments:

$$A\flat \ (IIx \text{-} V \ / \ III \text{-} \ \flat IIIx \ / \ II \text{-} \ \flat IIx \ / \ ) \text{ etc.}$$
$$A\flat \ (IIx \text{-} V \ / \ III \text{-} \ \flat IIIx \ / \ II \text{-} \ \flat IIx \ / \ ) \text{ etc.}$$

The following patterns with their usual points will assist the student in arriving at a" setting" for a tune:

A♭ I III // B II V / I / B VIIx ♭VIIx / VI ♭V∅ // A♭ IIx V / A♭ III ♭IIIx / II ♭IIx // etc.

NOTE: this pattern could be assigned the following points:

$$
\begin{array}{ccccc}
7 & 7 & 3 & 7 & 3 \\
I \text{-} & VI \text{-} & II \text{-} & V \text{-} & I \ \text{(See Fig. 1)}
\end{array}
$$

This, however, would create a whole-step movement in the *top voice*
in VI to II, which is weak, and no movement in II to V, which should be avoided. Fig. 3 is preferable. (See Fig. 2)

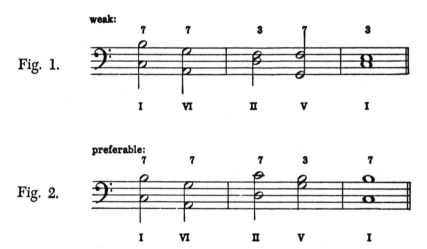

Fig. 1.

Fig. 2.

Fig. 3 is a bass line for "You Go To My Head" in A♭. Note the key changes. Improvise on Fig. 3.

Fig. 3.

YOU GO TO MY HEAD —

DRILL: Since this tune is usually played as a ballad, apply the same principles suggested in drill of lesson 42.

George Shearing

LESSON 44.

Block Chords

The appearance of the George Shearing Quintet in 1949 was the signal for a new major development in jazz piano. Shearing revealed a deep understanding of previous developments in the history of jazz piano. His major keyboard influences were Wilson, Tatum, and Powell. Like Powell, he had abandoned the swing-bass mannerisms of Wilson and Tatum in favor of the half-note harmonic unit in the left hand, and the rhythmic eighth-note line in the right.

Because Shearing has usually been supported by a full rhythm section, including a guitar, his left hand structures have usually appeared in a higher register of the piano (see Fig. 1).

Fig. 1.

Generally, Shearing has preferred an architecture similar to that studied in SECTION II rather than the seventh-third architecture of Powell.

Shearing's right hand single line is distinctly rooted in Powell's conception, although his right hand register avoids the area above high C (see Fig. 2)

Fig. 2.

However, the Shearing "sound" is usually associated with the block chords or "locked" hands architecture. This sound was utilized in a primitive manner by Milt Buckner in the middle Forties. Both Shearing and Buckner probably borrowed the sound from the Glenn Miller saxophone section. The normal instrumentation of most previous saxophone sections was two altos and two tenors. Miller introduced a fifth voice, a third tenor or a clarinet (top voice) to allow for the melody to be played in two voices an octave apart, with three inner voices (see Fig. 3).

Fig. 3.

This is the basis for the Shearing "sound," which will be analyzed in succeeding chapters. Transferred to the keyboard, these octave "blocks" are played with the bottom voice in the left hand, the four remaining voices in the right. This sound remains one of the great architectural innovations in the history of jazz piano and has become one of the permanent vernacular idioms employed by all jazz pianists today.

Fig. 4 is a bass line for "I Got Rhythm" to be explored in 12 keys.

Fig. 4.

I VI / II IVo / III ♭IIIo / II ♭IIx / I Ix₂ / II₄ IIφ₄ / VI₂ V♯³ /

I+⁶ ♯I / I VI / II IVo / III ♭IIIo / II ♭IIx / I Ix₂ / II₄ IIφ₄ /

VI₂ V♯³ / I+⁶ IVx / IIIx VIIm₄ / Vo IIIx₆ / VIx III₄ / Io VIx₆ /

IIx VI₄ / IVo IIx₆ / V II₄ / ♯VIo V₆ / I VI / II IVo / III ♭IIIo /

II ♭IIx / I Ix₂ / II₄ IIφ₄ / VI₂ IVo / IIIφ ♭IIIx / IIx ♭IIx / I+⁶ //

DRILL: Review Section VI, Volume I, in preparation for the succeeding material.

The Five Qualities

Since the block chord style is primarily used in playing melodies, several problems are raised. First, copyright laws prevent the reproduction of a melody; in addition, the five qualities must be presented before any practical application can be achieved. This chapter will present the block chords for the five qualities in twelve keys. Original melodies will be used as models.

Since melodies tend to follow the scales or modes of the prevailing chord, the simple principle here is one of playing the melody in octaves while adding three appropriate inner voices within the octave tones.

On this basis, the various modes originating on C would appear in chord blocks as in Fig. 1. This figure employs the following modes (see Section VI, Volume I):

QUALITY	MODE
Major	Ionian
Dominant	Mixolydian
Minor	Dorian
Half-diminished	Locrian
Diminished	0 2 1 2 1 2 1 2 1 (semitone combination)

In each case, except diminished, the signature of the prevailing mode has been used.

Fig. 1.

C Major (Ionian of C)

C Dominant (Mixolydian of F)

C Minor (Dorian of B♭)

C Half-diminished (Locrian of D♭)

C Diminished (0 2 1 2 1 2 1 2 1)

Fig. 1 illustrates a visually convenient way of presenting the chord blocks on the various modes; however, this multi-keyed presentation would be highly impractical in dealing with a single-key melody. Avoiding this problem for the moment, Fig. 2 presents the remaining block chords in their correct modal setting.

Fig. 2.

D♭ Major (Ionian of D♭)

Db Dominant (Mixolydian of Gb)

C# Minor (Dorian of B)

C# Half-diminished (Locrian of D)

C# Diminished (0 2 1 2 1 2 1 2 1)

D Major (Ionian of D)

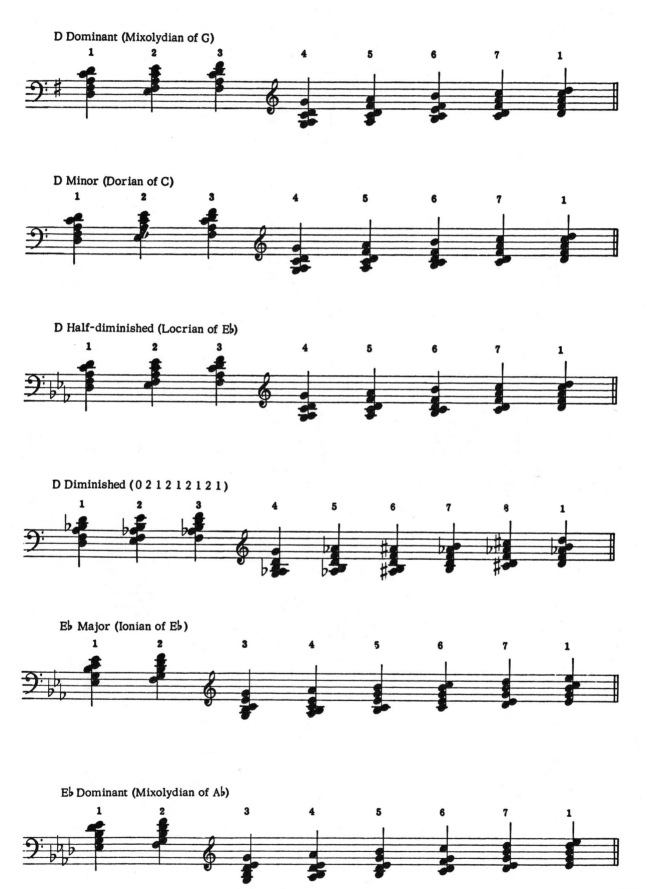

E♭ Minor (Dorian of D♭)

D♯ Half-diminished (Locrian of E)

E♭ Diminished (0 2 1 2 1 2 1 2 1)

E Major (Ionian of E)

E Dominant (Mixolydian of A)

E Minor (Dorian of D)

E Half-diminished (Locrian of F)

E Diminished (0 2 1 2 1 2 1 2 1)

F Major (Ionian of F)

F Dominant (Mixolydian of B♭)

F Minor (Dorian of E♭)

F Half-diminished (Locrian of G♭)

F Diminished (0 2 1 2 1 2 1 2 1)

F♯ Major (Ionian of F♯)

F♯ Dominant (Mixolydian of B)

F# Minor (Dorian of E)

F# Half-diminished (Locrian of G)

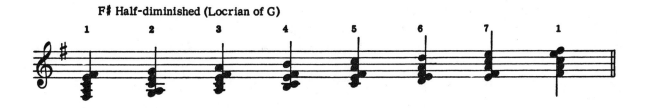

F# Diminished (0 2 1 2 1 2 1 2 1)

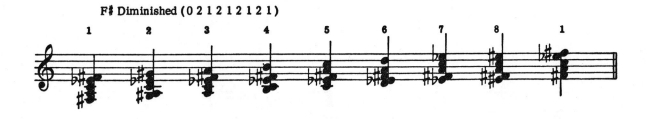

G Major (Ionian of G)

G Dominant (Mixolydian of C)

G Minor (Dorian of F)

G Half-diminished (Locrian of A♭)

G Diminished (0 2 1 2 1 2 1 2 1)

A♭ Major (Ionian of A♭)

A♭ Dominant (Mixolydian of D♭)

A♭ Minor (Dorian of G♭)

G♯ Half-diminished (Locrian of A)

G♯ Diminished (0 2 1 2 1 2 1 2 1)

A Major (Ionian of A)

A Dominant (Mixolydian of D)

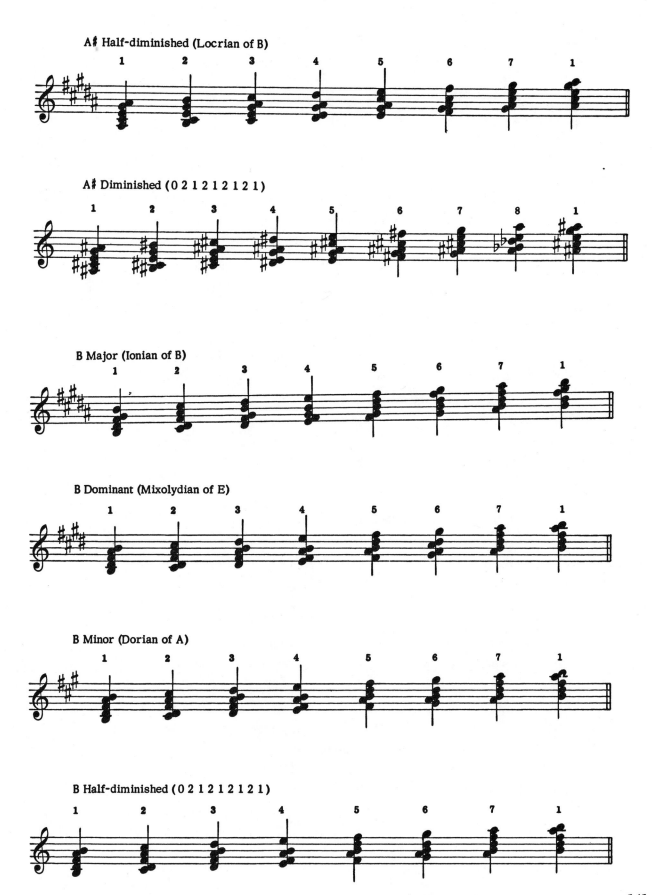

B Diminished (0 2 1 2 1 2 1 2 1)

The student will notice the presence of several *awkward* positions (both technical and auditory):

Mode	Position
M	4
x	4
m	4
m	6

These positions are seldom used melodically; the voicings are the closest approximation possible while retaining the prevailing quality.

All the positions in Figs. 1 and 2 follow basic rules:

1. Except in position 2 of all five qualities and position 6 of the dominant, the root always appears in the chord block.

2. In the excepted positions indicated in Step 1, the THIRD and SEVENTH appear in the block.

3. Except in position 6, the DIMINISHED FIFTH always appears in half-diminished and diminished blocks.

In the diminished voicings, the student will note that the inner voices for positions 1, 3, 5, and 7, respectively, also appear in positions 2, 4, 6, and 8.

DRILL: Study the modal chord blocks in Figs. 1 and 2 for automatic facility, abandoning reference to the printed page as soon as possible. In Figs. 1 and 2, four tones appear in the right hand, one in the left hand at all times.

LESSON 46.

The Melodic Positions

A melody may be defined, in jazz terms, as a series of tones moving through a pre-arranged sequence of modes. In any case, the melody in part derives its vitality from its relationship to the root of the prevailing chord and its implied mode. The problem here is to find the quickest device for arriving at the correct voicing.

The following tables can be an aid in this direction, although the student is advised to depend upon the principles described on page 130 for the solution — the tables are only to be used for occasional reference.

Each of the tables is based upon the prevailing mode of each chord — by now a familiar frame for the student.

MAJOR (*IONIAN*)

L. H.	R. H.
1	3 5 6 1
2	3 5 7 2
3	5 6 1 3
4	5 6 1 4
5	6 1 3 5
6	1 3 5 6
7	1 3 5 7
1	3 5 6 1

DOMINANT (*MIXOLYDIAN*)

L. H.	R. H.
1	3 5 7 1
2	3 5 7 2
3	5 7 1 3
4	5 7 1 4
5	7 1 3 5
6	7 2 3 6 *
7	1 3 5 7
1	3 5 7 1

MINOR (*DORIAN*)

L. H.	R. H.
1	3 5 7 1
2	3 5 7 2
3	5 7 1 3
4	5 7 1 4
5	7 1 3 5
6	7 1 3 6
7	1 3 5 7
1	3 5 7 1

HALF-DIMINISHED (*LOCRIAN*)

L. H.	R. H.
1	3 5 7 1
2	3 5 7 2
3	5 7 1 3
4	5 7 1 4
5	7 1 3 5
6	7 1 3 6
7	1 3 5 7
1	3 5 7 1

DIMINISHED (0 2 1 2 1 2 1 2 1)

L. H.	R. H.
1	3 5 7 1
2	3 5 7 2
3	5 7 1 3
4	5 7 1 4
5	7 1 3 5
6	7 1 3 6
7	1 3 5 7
8	1 3 5 8
1	3 5 7 1

As we have learned in Lesson 20, the 6 in a dominant chord becomes a thirteenth which usually is supported by a ninth; hence the 2 (ninth) in this voicing.

Each one of these voicings represents a melodic position possible on any one of the sixty chords. In Fig. 1, the numbers appearing over each melody note represent the position of each note in the prevailing mode of the chord.

Steps:

1. Assign a number to each melody note indicating its position in the prevailing mode of the chord.

2. Determine the table to be used by the *quality* of the chord underneath.

3. Find the position in the table and build a voicing on the prevailing mode of the chord, not the key of the tune.

Apply these steps to Fig. 1.

BAR	TABLE	PREVAILING KEY	MODE	POINT
1	M	C	Ionian	5-6-7-1
2	x	F	Mixolydian	2-7-1-2
3	φ	G♭	Locrian	7-5-3-5
4	m	E♭	Dorian	7-5-3-7
5	m	D	Dorian	7-5-3-4
6	m	G	Dorian	2-3-4-5
7	o	——	021212121	3-1-7-5
8	M	D♭	Ionian	7-7-6-5
9	M	C	Ionian	5

Fig. 1.

See Fig. 2.

Fig. 2.

Fig. 3 illustrates the melody and bass line of an original tune. Each melody tone has been assigned its **position** as related to the prevailing mode of the chord. The student should try for a "solution" to Fig. 3.

146

In Fig. 4, the inner voices have been added, keeping four tones in the right hand, and one in the left.

Fig. 4.

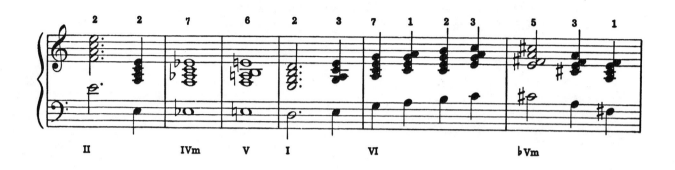

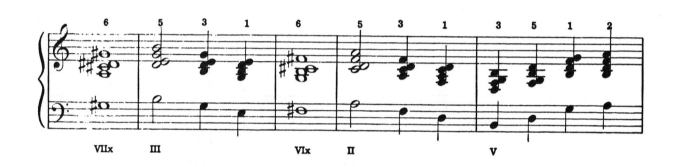

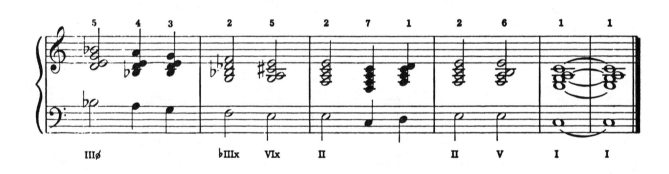

DRILL: Extract a melody from sheet music. Work out a harmonic solution, assign melodic positions and build the appropriate chord blocks. (See Lesson 76, Volume I.) *For now, play the open octaves on tones not appearing in the mode of the prevailing chord.* This subject will be discussed in Lesson 47.

Chromatic Melodic Positions

Occasionally, a melodic tone falls on a note not appearing in the prevailing mode. The solution to this is quite simple — as in dealing with the modal melodic positions, play the melodic tone with its octave, adding the available inner voices and keeping in mind the importance of the root third and seventh in all qualities, the fifth in half-diminished and diminished.

One helpful device is to explore the modal positions on either side of the chromatic position, raising or lowering the outside voices until an agreeable solution is found. The following tables illustrate the usual non-modal positions and their best solutions:

M: ♯4   Fig. 1.
   ♯5

x: ♭2 (♭9)
  ♯2 (♯9)
  ♭5   Fig. 2.
  ♭6 (♭13)

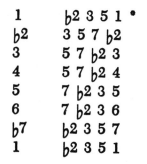

A common chromatic tone appearing in the dominant chord as an inner voice is the *flatted ninth* (♭2). Fig. 3 illustrates the melodic positions for the C dominant chord employing the flatted ninth. The voicing table is as follows, based on the *Mixolydian* mode.

1	♭2 3 5 1 *
♭2	3 5 7 ♭2
3	5 7 ♭2 3
4	5 7 ♭2 4
5	7 ♭2 3 5
6	7 ♭2 3 6
♭7	♭2 3 5 7
1	♭2 3 5 1

The seventh is usually omitted here to avoid a cluttered sound.

Fig. 3.

The student should explore the series in Fig. 3 on the remaining eleven dominant chords.

The *flatted thirteenth* (♭6) is often joined with the flatted ninth (♭2), Fig. 4.

Fig. 4.

Cx♭9

In Fig. 3 above, the positions of ♭2, 3, 5, and 7 forming "false diminished" chords are sometimes incorrectly referred to as diminished ninths. Evaluating these chords on the basis of the C root, they can only be dominant. The non-modal m, ø and o points are:

m: ♯1   Fig. 5.
    ♯7

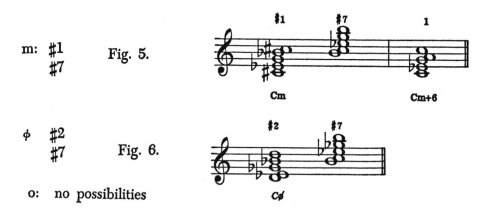

ø   ♯2
     ♯7   Fig. 6.

o: no possibilities

All illustrations in this lesson are of course based on the prevailing mode of the chord.

Fig. 7 is an original melody and chord chart illustrating the chromatic tones discussed in this chapter. Add the inner voices as in Lesson 46.

Fig. 7.

Note: the inversion in bar 11 in no way affects the voicing required by VI.
Fig. 8 is the solution.

Fig. 8.

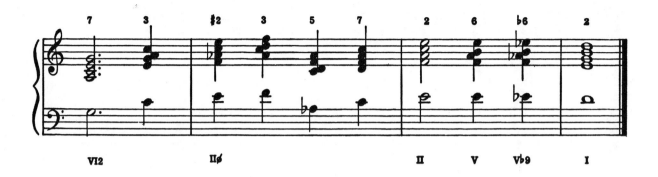

DRILL: Extract a melody from sheet music, work out a harmonic solution, and build voicings on melodic positions.

LESSON **48.**

Solo Block Chords

The block chord technique, both in the Miller band and as transferred to the keyboard by Shearing, has been a melodic device superimposed over a bass line. In this chapter we will attempt to add the root of each chord as a second voice in the left hand.

Fig. 1 illustrates a melodic fragment with the roots added in the left hand. The principle illustrated here is simply one of adding the root in the fifth finger of the left hand while following the melody line in the left hand, with the thumb and index finger. The right hand will continue to carry the remaining four tones; altogether, a six-voice system.

The problem here is to keep the root as far from the melody blocks as the individual hand span of the student will allow. For instance, span permitting, the first two bars of Fig. 1 will *sound* better if played as in Fig. 2. Here the depth of the roots adds a sonority missing in Fig. 1. The student should strive to utilize the deepest roots possible without, of course, "breaking" the chord.

Fig. 1.

Fig. 2.

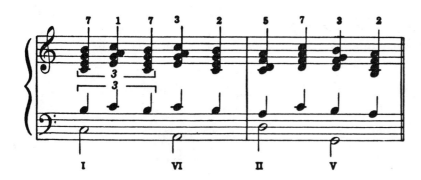

These supported voicings are an acceptable solo sound; they may also offer an area of individual exploration for the student in building his own choice of "architectural sounds."

Fig. 3 illustrates a common problem in "blocking" a melodic line, the melodic tones often "run over" from one chord to another. This requires an adjustment of both the inner voices and the root, while leaving the melodic tones undisturbed.

Fig. 3.

In Fig. 4 the tied chords require two beats on II and one on IIφ, the remaining quarter-note chord is also a IIφ.

Fig. 4.

Here the inner voice (*in this case the fifth*) moves to the new quality on the third beat of the bar while leaving the melodic tones, the root, and the remaining inner voices undisturbed.

In cases in which I moves to VI, inner voice adjustment is not usually necessary; the new root, of course, must be introduced.

Fig. 5 is a bass line for "The Nearness of You" in F. The roots to be played with the melodic block chords appear in the bass clef.

Fig. 5.

THE NEARNESS OF YOU — by Ned Washington and Hoagy Carmichael
Copyright © 1937 and 1940 by Famous Music Corporation
Used by permission.

DRILL:

1. Transfer the melody from the sheet music to manuscript paper.

2. Add the roots in the bass clef; place Roman numerals below.

3. Assign melodic *positions* on the basis of prevailing modes.

4. Add chord blocks, playing the roots with fifth finger of the left hand.

The student is advised to avoid the melodic syncopation appearing in sheet music on the first and third beats of the bars in order to start the melodic phrases with the prevailing chords.

Block Chords With Inversions

As pointed out in a note in Lesson 47 (Fig. 7), the presence of an inversion symbol refers only to the root to be played by the fifth finger of the left hand; it in no way affects the right hand block which takes its construction from the Roman numerals only.

Fig. 1 illustrates a set of chord blocks built on an inversion line with the bass notes appearing in the left hand. Melodic *positions* are determined on the basis of the Roman numeral; *the inversion does not affect the position.*

Fig. 1.

Fig. 2 is a bass line for "Flamingo" in E♭.

Fig. 2.

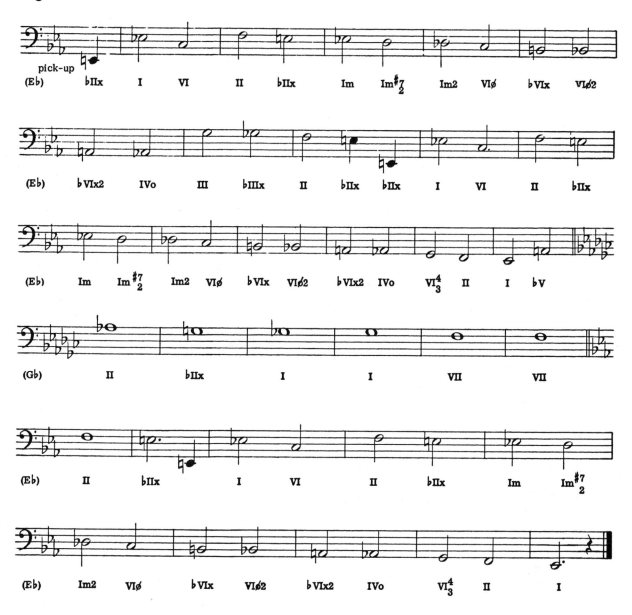

DRILL: Extract melody from sheet music. Add bass notes in bass clef.
Place Roman numerals below. Assign melodic "points" based on
the *prevailing mode of the Roman numeral — not the inversion.*
Add block chords.

LESSON **50.**

Minor Scale — Tone Block Chords

The minor scale-tone seventh chords were thoroughly studied in Section X, Volume I. Fig. 1 illustrates the minor scale-tone seventh chords in c minor. As in all keys, the minor scale-tone seventh chords contain the following qualities:

Position	Chord	Symbol
I	— minor large seventh	mL
II	— half-diminished seventh	φ
III	— major augmented seventh	M+
IV	— minor seventh	m
V	— dominant seventh	x
VI	— half-diminished seventh	φ
VII	— diminished seventh	o

Fig. 1.

Figs. 2 and 3 illustrate the melodic *position* for the minor large and major augmented seventh chords.

Fig. 2.

Fig. 3.

Fig. 2 is based upon the Ionian mode (1 - 1) of the ascending melodic minor scale on C. Fig. 4.

Fig. 4.

Fig. 3 is based upon the Phrygian mode (3 - 3) of the same scale. Fig. 5.

Fig. 5.

Fig. 6 is a bass line for "Lullaby of the Leaves" in C minor. The student should note the harmonic complexity in this line. The c minor "front section" dissolves into C major in the "bridge", then returns to c minor through a deceptive cadence in bar 24. The student is advised to study the minor scale-tone chords in all keys. See Section X, Volume I.

Fig. 6.

(c) I+6 ♭IIM   I+6 Im2 (C) ♭VIx   ♭VIx   I   II   III   VI

(C) ♭VIx   ♭VIx   III ♭IIIx (c) II ♭IIx   I+6   VI   II   V♭9

(c) Vm ♭V   IV IV2   II V♭9   II ♭IIx   I+6   I+6

DRILL: Complete the chord blocks for Fig. 6.

LESSON 51.

Right Hand Chord Blocks

As indicated in the beginning of this section, block chords are traditionally played with four tones in the right hand, one in the left. However, in adding the root to the left hand, as in Lessons 48, 49, and 50, the awkward problem of simultaneously playing the melody in both hands, can sometimes be relieved by placing the entire block in the right hand. This will permit the left hand to extend the roots deeper into the bass.

Some students will find the playing of all five voices of the block chord in the right hand beyond their span. However, much of this idiom is within an average span and for this reason has been included.

Fig. 1 is a bass line for "Stardust" in D♭.

Fig. 1.

STAR DUST—
Copyright 1929 by Mills Music, Inc.
Used by permission.

DRILL: Extract the melody from the sheet music. Assign *positions* to each melodic tone in relation to the prevailing mode. Add blocks to the right hand. For those whose hand span does not allow the playing of all the tones in each block, it is suggested that the outer voices be played, along with those inner voices within reach.

Block Chords — "Walking" Bass Lines

"Walking" bass lines refer to the quarter note scale-arpeggio lines played by bass players in modern jazz groups. As described in Lesson 34, Volume I, the unique quality of jazz lies in a particular combination of rhythmic elements:

eighth-notes — melodic time
half-note — harmonic time
quarter-note — rhythmic time

In pianistic terms, this may be illustrated as follows:
eighth-note — right hand
half-note — left hand
quarter-note — foot beat

These rhythmic elements usually prevail in modern "group" piano. However, it is possible to re-arrange these elements in order to create an acceptable solo sound in modern rhythmic terms (avoiding swing bass).

Bassists utilize the identical tonal devices described in Volume I: arpeggios, scales, modes, scale fragments, and chromatic tones. Rhythmically, however, the bassist is generally assigned to the quarter note, in order to establish a firm rhythmic underpinning for the piano and the various horns (wind instruments).

We will return to this aspect of jazz in Volume IV; for now we will attempt to join this walking line with the block chord technique in the right hand.

Fig. 1 is a "walking" bass line for "September in the Rain." Proceed as in previous lessons playing the available chord blocks in the right hand.

Fig. 1.

SEPTEMBER IN THE RAIN —
Copyright 1937 by Remick Music Corporation
Used by permission.

note: The ninth of the half-diminished chord, unlike the major, dominant minor and diminished, does not fall in the prevailing mode.

DRILL: Construct a walking line on a previous bass line or one converted from sheet music and apply melodic chord blocks in the right hand.

LESSON 53.

Improvised Chord Blocks

Shearing not only developed the block chord technique to present a melody and its accompanying harmony simultaneously, he also employed the block chord in his improvised line, substituting a quick succession of chord blocks for the exclusively single note line used by Powell (see Fig. 1: *Powell*; Fig. 2: *Shearing*).

Fig. 1.

Fig. 2.

In Fig. 3 the student will note that blocks do not appear on every melodic tone but only on the important tones of the phrases falling on any one of the eight melodic positions in the bar. This device is employed in rapid passages to give the illusion of continuous block sounds without the awkward necessity of playing a complete five tone block on each melodic tone. If the student attempts to play Fig. 2 at a rapid tempo, it will be evident that the natural swing of the phrase is diminished; it is to avoid this that the open octave is employed.

Fig. 3.

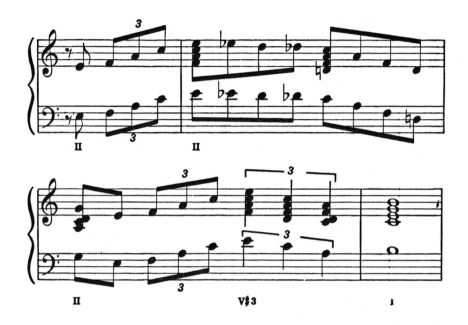

The basic principle of improvised lines employing block chords is as follows: *The improvised line is played in octaves employing both hands; chord blocks are introduced at the accent points in a phrase.*

Fig. 4 is an improvised block chord line on "Don't You Know I Care" in Eb.

Fig. 4.

DON'T YOU KNOW I CARE —

DRILL: Explore other improvised lines inserting chord blocks in all accented positions.

SECTION V
Horace Silver

LESSON 54.

General

Much like a serious composer, the jazz musician critically selects the specific tonal and rhythmic elements which best serve his aesthetic purposes.

The essential problem confronted by Wilson and Tatum was one of harnessing the blues-ragtime traditions to a classical technique in order to expand the expressive gamut of jazz piano.

Powell returned to the "horn" tradition, transforming the lines of Coleman Hawkins, Lester Young, and Charlie Parker to the keyboard as Hines transformed Armstrong fifteen years earlier.

Shearing continued to expand the expressive texture of the piano while securely establishing the "horn" concept of contemporary jazz piano.

Horace Silver, the next important link in the history of modern jazz piano, has, like his predecessors, effected major contributions in the vital areas of techniques, architecture, and aesthetics. These aspects of Silver's achievement will be discussed in the remaining lessons of this Volume as well as sections of Volume IV.

Fig. 3 illustrates a bass line for "Falling In Love With Love" in B♭. Fig. 1 illustrates a conversion of 3/4 to 4/4 time discussed in Volume I, Lesson 71. In the case of "Tenderly" in Volume I, a 4/4 conversion was accomplished by adding one beat to the first beat of each bar. In the case of "Falling In Love With Love" this device will function, but the resulting 4/4 chart is an awkward 64 bar harmonization containing extended cadences of the V and I chord, which diminishes the "swing" of the conversion.

Fig. 1.

I / I / ♯Io / ♯Io / II / II / V / V / III / ♭IIIx / II / ♭IIx /
I / I / ♭IIx / ♭IIx / I / I / IV / IV / etc.

In a case of this type, the process described in Lesson 71, Vol. I is REVERSED. This means that instead of adding one beat to each bar, one beat is *removed* from each bar. See Fig. 2 for melodic conversion.

Fig. 2.

Fig. 3.

4/4 conversion

I / #Io / II / V / III ♭IIIx / II ♭IIx / I / ♭IIx / I / IV /

VIIm / ♭VIIx / VI#♯⁷ VI⁷ / VI ♭IIIo / II / ♭IIx / I / #Io /

II / V / III ♭IIIx / II ♭IIx / I / ♭IIx / I / IV / VIIm IIIx /

III∅ VIx / IV⁺⁶ III / II ♭IIx / I⁺⁶ / I⁺⁶ //

DRILL: Attempt conversion of other 3/4 tunes. In each case either a
beat must be ADDED to each bar or REMOVED from each bar.
The student should decide upon the most effective solution.

LESSON 55.

Technique

Silver's technical innovations stem from the curious fact that at the
time of his initial achievement he was not a skilled pianist by existing
standards. It was this very fact that led to his "unpianistic" innovations.
These innovations consisted of a muscular, legato wrist stroke which simu-
lated the sharp attack of the tenor saxophone, his major instrument prior
to 1949.

In preparation for this "articulated" stroke, the following studies are suggested:

1. Practice the 12 major scales employing a rapid wrist stroke, with alternate hands. (see Fig. 1). Avoid "air-space" between notes.

Fig. 1.

2. Practice step 1 using the Hanon studies in 12 keys.

3. Practice Step 1 with the sixty scales (modes).

An important aspect of these studies is the *equal ability of each of the five fingers to support the full weight of the arm.* In modern jazz phrasing the accented arm weight often falls on the fourth or fifth finger (see Fig. 2), which makes this principle of equal finger strength essential.

Fig. 2.

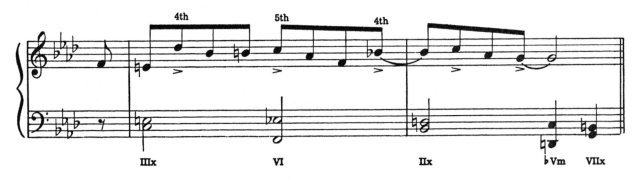

Fig. 3 is a bass line for "One For the Road."

Fig. 3.

pick-up

(E♭) ♭IIx // I II₂ / I ♭IIx / I II₂ / I II₂ / I II₂ / I ♭IIx / I Vm /

(E♭) Ix ♭V / IV Vm₂ / IV ♭VIIx / I II / ♯IIo III / IIIx♯⁵ VIx /

(E♭) II ♭IIM / I⁺⁶ VI // (G) IIø ♭IIx / I II₂ / I ♭IIx /

(G) I II₂ / I II₂ / I II₂ / I ♭IIx / I Vm / Ix ♭V / IV Vm₂ /

(G) IV ♭VIIx / I II / ♯IIo III / IIIx♯⁵ VIx / II ♭IIM / I⁺⁶ ♭VIx /

(G) Vm ♭V / IVx Im / IVx IVm / III VI ♭VIx / Vm ♭V / IVx Im /

(G) IVx / ♭III ♭VIx / V♯³ ♭IIx / I II₂ / I ♭IIx / I II₂ / I II₂ /

(G) I II₂ / I ♭IIx / I Vm / Ix ♭V / IV Vm₂ / IV ♭VIIx / I II /

(G) ♯IIo III / IIIx♯⁵ VIx / II V♯³ / ♭VIIx VIx / ♭VIx V /

(G) I⁺⁶ / I⁺⁶ //

ONE FOR MY BABY (AND ONE MORE FOR THE ROAD) —
by Howard Arlen and Johnny Mercer
Edwin Morris & Company, Inc.
Used by permission.

DRILL: The student is advised at this point to begin a serious study of pages 122 to 128, Volume II, which notates the entire "Opus de Funk." This improvisation, recorded in the early Fifties, represented a revolutionary development in the history of jazz piano. This recorded solo clearly illustrates the basic characteristics of Silver's style. Also, a stunning discography of Silver dating back to 1950 is suggested as a valuable source of study of this outstanding musician.

DRILL: Analyze "Opus de Funk" for the following:
1. "Peak" positions of phrases in each bar to determine accent points.
2. Fingering of phrases, employing normal fingering rules, to determine arm-weight points in each bar.
3. Punctuation of phrases to determine melodic "contours."

LESSON 56.

Architecture

Bud Powell firmly established a left hand architecture based upon the 3-7-3 concept. Shearing's left hand architecture is of little formal significance in the format of the quintet, since the underpinning of the group is well distributed between drums, bass, piano, and guitar.

Silver has maintained the basic Powell architecture, although he has brought a rhythmic punctuation to the style not present in the more legato Powell idiom. More important, Silver established new dynamic and expressive levels with the right hand. This has allowed for the interplay of contrapuntal lines between the hands, an important aspect of the 3-7-3 concept in contemporary jazz piano.

Fig. 1.

Silver's basic right hand register is illustrated in Fig. 1. This allows the "horn line" to be played in the middle area of the keyboard instead of the less intense upper area. The eighth note is the basic unit of the highly accented line, the accent falling on constantly shifting points (eight to a bar). These accent points preponderantly fall on the top note of the phrase, which invariably places the accent on the fourth or fifth finger (see Fig. 2).

Fig. 2.

Tacit　　　　　　　　　　　Tacit

Fig. 3 is a bass line for "The Breeze And I" in D.

I^{+6} / I / I / I^{+6} / Vϕ / Vϕ / III $\flat$IIIx / II $\flat$IIx / I^{+6} / I / I /

I^{+6} / Vϕ / Vϕ / I / VI / II / V$^{\sharp 3}$ / III / VI / II / $\flat$IIx / I /

$\sharp$Io / II / V$^{\sharp 3}$ / III / VI / II / $\flat$IIx / I^{+6} / Vϕ / I^{+6} / I^{+6} //

LESSON 57.

The Blues Tradition

The joining of the African beat with the many facets of our culture (popular, classical, theatrical, religious), resulted in the emergence of a new exciting art form — jazz.

These joinings first appeared in a variety of forms: work songs, field hollers, blues, folk songs, rags, marches, dances, chanties, and spirituals.

In each period, these basic sub-strata elements are "rediscovered" and revised to fit the new conceptions of rhythm and harmony.

Silver has performed this service by returning to the blues-folk-spiritual tradition, and revising these idioms in terms of post-bop ideas.

Integrated into the "modern horn" line we find the following revised elements:

1. "Blue" notes. 2. Crushed tones.

The following tables illustrate the "blue" or *non-modal* tones for each of the five quailties:

Major: ♯1   ♯2   ♯4   ♯5   ♯6
Dominant: ♯1   ♯2   ♯4   ♯5   ♯7

Minor: ♯1   ♯3   ♯4   ♯5   ♯7
Half-diminished: ♯2   ♯3   ♯5   ♯6   ♯7
Diminished: ♯1   ♯3   ♯5   ♯7

(all figures based on prevailing mode of the chord).

As described in Lesson 61, Volume I, the *crushed tones* are derived from the tradition of folk guitar. In addition to the material described in Volume I, the following is a basic underlying principle of the *crushed tone* technique:

The fifth finger in the right hand is placed and held upon the tonic of the prevailing key of the tune, while a moving lower voice is played in the lower part of the hand. This lower voice usually centers about the third, fourth, of the prevailing tonic (Ionian) mode in addition to the surrounding chromatic tones. The student should keep in mind that this technique is not determined by the quality or position of the immediate chord, only by the prevailing key or tonic of the tune. See Fig. 1 noting each prevailing tonic (signature). Of course in tunes involving modulation to a new key, the tonic of the new key will prevail.

This feeling is by no means limited to the 12 bar blues, but is an all embracing quality which should be present in any jazz performance.

Fig. 1 illustrates this technique applied to several keys by various jazz pianists.

Fig. 1.

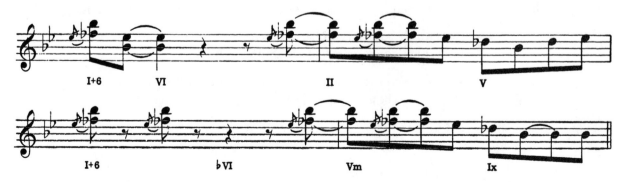

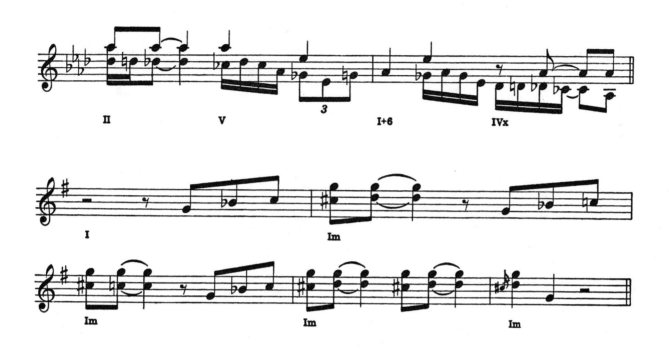

DRILL: Explore the 12 bar blues in 12 keys (see Lesson 32), applying
this technique to the right hand line.